Michael Wood is a highly respected author and TV presenter. He has over eighty documentary films to his name, most recently the critically acclaimed *The Story of India*. He is a Fellow of the Royal Historical Society.

THE
GREAT TURNING POINTS
IN BRITISH HISTORY

The 20 events that made the nation

INTRODUCTION BY MICHAEL WOOD

Constable • London

CONSTABLE

First published in the UK by Constable, an imprint
of Constable & Robinson Ltd., 2009

Reprinted in 2016 by Constable

3 5 7 9 10 8 6 4 2

Copyright © BBC History Magazine, 2009

The moral right of the author has been asserted.

A CIP catalogue record for this book
is available from the British Library.

ISBN: 978-1-84529-927-9

Printed and bound in Great Britain by Clays Ltd, St Ives plc

Papers used by Constable are from well-managed forests
and other responsible sources

MIX
Paper from
responsible sources
FSC® C104740

Constable
An imprint of
Little, Brown Book Group
Carmelite House
50 Victoria Embankment
London EC4Y 0DZ

An Hachette UK Company
www.hachette.co.uk

www.littlebrown.co.uk

CONTENTS

Foreword

DAVID MUSGROVE

What are the twenty key years in the last millennium of British history? That was the question I set out to resolve when I started commissioning the Turning Points series for *BBC History Magazine* in the closing months of 2005. I asked twenty leading historians to pick the year that they considered to have the most significance in a given half-century, to nominate the one year that they thought was the turning point for that particular fifty-year period.

Of course, there are several problems with this. First, as Michael Wood goes some way to countering in his Introduction, is the arbitrary starting date of AD 1000. British history clearly does not commence in this year and by taking this as our starting point we miss much of significance prior to that. We hear nothing of Romans arriving, occupying and leaving, Celts surviving and prospering, Anglo-Saxons finding their new home, Christianity spreading across the islands, Vikings invading and settling, not to mention the long swath of silent prehistory that goes before all that. Clearly this is something of an oversight, but it is worth saying that the further back in time one treks, the more difficult it becomes to ascribe events to specific years and thus the harder this particular task becomes.

The second issue is whether years can actually be ascribed as turning points. History is as much about trends as events, so aren't we distorting the past by trying to shoehorn the wider themes of the past into critical years? That is a valid criticism, but every trend has a pivot point, so it is perfectly acceptable to try and pluck out that moment. Trends aside, sometimes history does turn on the big moments; set-piece battles do lead to regime change, new charters and laws do transform the political landscape, and virulent plagues do enforce dramatic alterations in the way society works.

Third, and perhaps most challenging, is the 'British' bit of the equation. The United Kingdom of Great Britain and Northern Ireland as we know it today is not much more than a century old. A large part of the story of the British Isles over the past thousand years is that of English attempts to dominate Wales, Ireland and Scotland. This makes things rather tricky. We have to contend with the fact that before the various political and dynastic unions, events of undeniable moment in one country might be rather less significant in the short term in another. The choice of the year when Magna Carta was signed (1215) for the period 1200–49 is a good case in point. In the immediate aftermath, the signing of the charter forced a change in John's kingship in England, but Scotland, Wales and Ireland did not feel the consequences of this significant step on the road to our modern sense of British liberty until much later, when the nations were bound together as one. In the end, however, that idea of a certain sort of liberty espoused at least in part at Magna Carta does permeate the British identity, and so an initially English event can be read as a British turning point. I realize I'm leaving myself open to accusations of Anglocentrism, so I would like to stress the point that I'm certainly not saying that what is important for England automatically becomes important for Britain, but there are cases where that applies.

Some of our turning points dwell specifically on this expansionist desire from England, and the English attempts to dominate and conquer abroad have clear-cut implications for the whole of Britain and its history, a good case in point being the 1171 invasion of Ireland, or 1285 and Edward's effort to consolidate his English rule in Wales. In these cases, the wider consequences for the whole of Britain are more immediately apparent.

Britishness today, of course, is a concept under some stress, with devolution and perhaps more on the agenda outside England, and immigration from Europe seemingly causing consternation in some quarters about a dilution of our national nature. Politicians seem constantly on the look-out for ways to open up debates about Britishness or to find ways to shore up what they appear to see as this faltering concept. It is interesting and pertinent, then, I hope, to look back at the years that have been of signal importance in creating the Britain that is being so widely and regularly discussed today.

It might seem to you that some of our contributors had an easier time than others with their fifty-year slice of history. Could Nick Higham have chosen anything other than 1066 for his slot, for instance? Probably not, given its iconic status in our national story, although I'm sure a good case could have been made for 1086 and the Domesday Book. To offset that, we have allowed our historians to hedge their bets slightly, by picking nine other key years. That no doubt helps those invited to write on half-centuries where the choice is not quite so immediately obvious. As we get closer to the present day, the task for the historian does seem to get ever harder. Is the pace of the past hotting up or are we just more familiar with the events?

Whichever it is, Catherine Hall's 1832 will be decried by some for missing the more obvious Trafalgar 1805, Waterloo 1815, and indeed the slavery abolition years within that half-century. Peter Mandler had a similarly taxing choice with 1850–99 and then Gerard DeGroot had an embarrassment of riches for his 1900–49 slot. Two world wars, one great depression and the creation of the NHS make for a hard decision. And then we must spare a thought for Pat Thane, who got the poisoned chalice of the last half-century of the last millennium. Her choice of Suez is eminently defensible, but she also had the Cold War to contend with, plus at the very end of her fifty years the moves to loosen the bounds of the United Kingdom, of which so much of the previous nineteen half-centuries were concerned with bringing together.

Introduction

MICHAEL WOOD

When it comes to turning points, I suspect nations are the same as people. When we look back over our own lives, each of us engages in a process of selection and interpretation, reshaping the story that gives meaning and value to the present, creating a picture of the past that enables us to act more confidently in the present. It is a process that also engages with those around us – family, neighbours and friends – so that our individual narrative finds its place and takes its strength from a sense of a shared past.

But here's the rub: our sense of the relative significance of events – our own personal turning points – can change radically over time. Things we thought significant when we were 19 look different at 30, and unrecognizable at 60. Relationships, events, triumphs and disasters that mattered a great deal back then, may find themselves no longer part of the narrative, while once insignificant or ignored factors may now loom much larger. We have all surely experienced the feeling of finally recognizing the significance of a long-past moment: '*Now* I understand . . .'

Nations are the same. The selection and choice (and the omission) of the great turning points of a nation's story often change with time. In a new country such as the US the selection of these key moments in the creation of nationhood is different from old countries such as Britain. The more history a nation has, the more dangerous the selection can be. The Elizabethans went back to their medieval roots, quarrying the Anglo-Saxon past for new interpretations of English Christianity and the Church of England. The Victorian imperial heyday was painted in medieval colours, which dressed the Saxons as virtuous lawmakers, noble warriors and benevolent Christians overlaid by a myth of Teutonic racial superiority that coloured the ethos of the late nineteenth-century imperium.

When I was a student in the late 1960s, on the other hand, it was the suppressed histories of social movements that heralded the new turning points in the development of our sense of citizenship and nationality. The exhumation of the forgotten radical groups of the seventeenth century, the Putney Debates or E.P. Thompson's *The Making of the English Working Class* were all the rage and changed the way we made our picture of the British past.

It didn't last long, of course. In Thatcher's Britain the pendulum swung the other way. A pamphlet on the teaching of history by Hugh Thomas had a preface, written by Mrs T. herself, explicitly rejecting E.P. Thompson's vision of 'Peoples' History', in favour of the revival of history as the discussion of great figures and significant events. I well remember filming Thompson at the Glastonbury Festival in the high tide of Thatcherism as he implored the vast crowd to remember that British history was 'not just the story of kings and queens and imperialists and capitalists, but of inventors and poets, of the Levellers and William Blake'.

All of which is to say that our view of the nation's turning points is always changing; this is what makes this impressive collection so timely and so fascinating.

Anyone interested in our history will want to dip into this intriguing and challenging set of twenty essays by top specialists spanning the last thousand years. There are many surprises. Half of the turning points, for example, are before 1500, which offers an enlightening long view of the nation's story rather than an over-concentration on recent events. Second, some of the selections are refreshingly unexpected. But all ask us to look at the very idea of turning points in a new light.

THE LONG AND THE SHORT OF IT

Most of the turning points within this book are about events, single moments in time in which the fate of the nation might seem to have turned on the flip of a coin. To some, though, these events are what Fernand Braudel memorably called 'surface ephemera . . . fireflies flitting across the surface of history'. To Braudel, these moments stood against the *longue durée* of climate, landscape, culture and society in all its deep-rooted attachments – the slow movement of real change within history.

In this light, the selection here of the Peasants' Revolt or the Great Reform Bill are moments that really stand as signifiers of wider social movements, markers in the long gradual rise of the ordinary people of Britain. These points can be found more often than expected. Intensive examination of our vast archives of medieval court rolls has revealed the reality of this hidden history. Such events do not constitute turning points in themselves, but they are part of the slow tidal movement of change. In this light, 'turning points' are perhaps not necessarily always initiators of change but they are visible signifiers of the crystallization of the wider historical process.

There is one last observation; one that has come up a lot

in recent debates over the national history curriculum. The greatest fact in our modern history is the British Empire and, it seems to me, the fact of the empire overshadows all else. Not long ago I argued in a public forum that the empire should be put at the centre of the school history curriculum. A number of commentators of Caribbean and African descent involved in the forum feared that this opinion verged on the racist. Not so. The empire is our common history; it is all our histories, whether we were passengers on the *Empire Windrush*, or came from India or Pakistan after Partition or, for that matter, are from Bede's Jarrow.

We all share the empire for good or ill: our schoolkids should be free to interrogate the attitudes (racist or not) of our forefathers as well as the altruism of the likes of, say, A.O. Hume, the founder of the Indian Congress. A writer such as Kipling may be disparaged in some quarters these days, but he is one of the half-dozen greatest writers in English: is it better to teach a second-rate writer who is politically correct, or a first-rate one who is problematic? In the classroom I'd take the problematic every time.

STARTING POINTS

This book covers a thousand-year span starting with the Danish Conquest of 1016. But of course there were many crucial developments in Britain before the eleventh century, especially in the national stories of the English, Welsh, Scots and Irish and their polities, languages and cultures in the post-Iron Age world. We could go much further back: to the core of our genetic makeup in the pre-Celtic population; to the arrival of migrants speaking early Indo-European languages; or to the Iron Age revolution in farming; and the coming of the Romans . . .

But let us limit our delving back in time to the five centuries before this book's starting point, the so-called Dark Ages, for this is the time when the cultural identities of the Scots, Welsh, Irish and English were first shaped. Here, then – as a prequel – are a suggested half-dozen significant turning points before the eleventh century.

First: the fall of Rome and the migration of Germanic migrants into Britain. This used to be called the *adventus Saxonum*, the 'coming of the English', and was long the centre of the English racial myth. It was even given a precise date (AD 449) and a place (Ebbsfleet by Richborough in Kent), as if this turning point was a single event. In fact, the arrival of the 'English' was a much slower process by relatively small numbers of Saxons, Angles, Jutes and Frisians over a long period of time. The new arrivals did not alter the deep DNA of Britain, but they had a profound effect on the languages, place names and institutions. Even today the Queen claims descent from a fifth-century 'Anglo-Saxon' adventurer called Cerdic, whose pagan burial mound lies on a windy hill above Andover. Cerdic's name, though, is not Old English but Celtic – a warning not to take historical myths too seriously!

My second turning point has a specific moment in time: AD 597, the coming of St Augustine with his evangelizing mission from Rome. Christianity had survived in Ireland, and in northern and western Britain, since the end of the Roman era, but the arrival of Augustine was a real moment of change. Strangely, the event attracted little attention on its 1,400th anniversary in 1997. Christianity is in steep decline now – recent polls suggest that England is the least religious society in the world – and in 1997 no one I read seemed to get a handle on why it mattered, but matter it did. It shaped English politics and culture and ways of thought for well over a thousand years. We can't begin to understand our ancestors without it, and not just our medieval forebears: take Shakespeare, for example, or the seventeen-century radicals. Christopher Hill, the great historian of the seventeenth century, always used to tell his students that if they didn't know the Bible they might as well give up trying to understand the Revolution! Augustine's arrival in 597 created the connection with Rome and European civilization that was tenaciously maintained for so long: it determined the path that our culture and civilization would take. That makes it one of the most important events in our history, though it may not appear so now because few of us take religion seriously any longer.

My third date is not so much a turning point as a landmark, a signpost: AD 731. In that year the Venerable Bede, a monk from the north of England, finished his *Ecclesiastical History of the English People*. The shape of early medieval English Christian culture was drawn by Bede in a lifetime's work, but this book defined Britain as a kind of heaven on earth, and England as an idea: it's the blueprint right down to Blake's Jerusalem. Bede's text was translated from the Latin into Old English by Alfred the Great and by Thomas Stapleton in the heated cultural politics of Tudor England. Stapleton prefaced his wonderfully vigorous version with a letter addressed to Elizabeth, begging her to read it as an exemplar of 'the true faith of Englishmen'.

My fourth Dark Age turning point is the Vikings, whose unwelcomed visitations were the catalyst for the creation of regional kingdoms in Wales, Scotland and England. Whether the unification of England would have happened without them is a moot question. So too perhaps for Rhodri Mawr's Wales and Kenneth MacAlpin's Alba (the forerunner of Scotland). In addition, the Vikings had a profound effect on society, kingship and even language in these islands. There is no specific date to pinpoint the Vikings' arrival: a medieval Canterbury tradition says the

Danes sacked Thanet in 753. The Anglo-Saxon Chronicle says the first attack was three ships on the Dorset coast in 789. But the key moment is the one seen as the turning point by a horrified contemporary, the great Northumbrian scholar Alcuin in AD 793: the sack of Lindisfarne, the great centre of Northumbrian monasticism. A resident in Charlemagne's Francia, Alcuin wrote, 'It is almost 350 years since we and our forefathers have dwelt in this fair land, and never before have such terrible things happened in Britain . . . Who could have thought such voyages could ever have been made?'

The Vikings would oversee the dismantling of the old order in Britain and they paved the way for the West Saxon creation of England. They also bring me to my fifth turning point: Alfred the Great. No other English ruler is called 'the Great' and that is how it should be. If the idea of England, the *gens Anglorum*, was Bede's, the English state was the creation of Alfred and his successors in the late ninth and early tenth centuries.

Alfred the man, however, is the key: in his struggle for survival when the war against the Danes was going against him; then in his subsequent dedication to the rebirth of law, social order, learning and literacy. Alfred in my view is the most remarkable figure in British history. But the England Alfred dreamed of was a family project pursued over several generations in a series of remarkable developments in state building, local organization, the construction of towns, the issuing of coinage and in the making of English law. The kingdom of England in reality was the work of three remarkable rulers: Alfred, his son Edward, and his grandson Æthelstan; together, arguably the most remarkable triad of rulers in British history.

Edward was ruthless and unsentimental, 'in learning far inferior to his father', wrote one chronicler, 'but far surpassing him in power and glory'. He is one medieval British ruler of whom we could hope to know much more, but probably never will. However, there have been many discoveries in recent years about his son Æthelstan – enough to show that he is one of the greatest figures in British history. In a society on a constant war footing, Æthelstan's reign saw a series of startling innovations. They didn't all work: his imperium was geographically overstretched; his law codes reflect the daunting gap between the ideal and reality in early medieval kingship ('frankly, a mess' was the verdict of the greatest modern expert, Patrick Wormald). Nonetheless his ambition, with a mitigating touch of humanity, still speaks to us.

The most famous event in Æthelstan's reign was the defeat of a huge coalition of Scots, Celts, Norse, Irish and Vikings at Brunanburh in 937. The battle has been celebrated in poems, songs, sagas and folktales for a thousand years; but, frustratingly, the site of this epic struggle has never been pinned down. It was chosen in a recent newspaper poll as one of the top ten decisive events of British history while *The Times*, a year or two back, announced the discovery of the site, the 'Birthplace of Britishness', in the Wirral. The site now has a monument and a Heritage History Trail, though it is perhaps more likely that Brunanburh remains undiscovered near the Humber.

Æthelstan established the idea of royal authority law and coinage over all the lands south of Humber, and a looser authority to the north: what medievalists call the *creation of an allegiance*; still a crucial thing today, this is what all governments aspire to since it is what lies at the root of all debates about identity and citizenship.

Therefore, if you want to take one great turning point date before the eleventh century, I choose AD 927, when the kingdom of England was created by Æthelstan. The creation of the early English state was a political and military act, accomplished by war, but fired by a big idea:

Bede's history of the *gens Anglorum*, the English people. Æthelstan had not been intended to be king of Wessex, but following the death of his half-brother, Ælfweard, the designated heir, he emerged as king out of a power struggle tilted by the Mercians, who saw Æthelstan (who had been raised in Mercia) as their man.

In early summer AD 927 Æthelstan overran Northumbria, captured York and called the northern British kings to a pact of mutual peace and protection at Dacre, Cumbria. That July a continental poet in his entourage sent a poem back to Winchester, remodelling verses originally addressed to Charlemagne, saluting 'this completed England' (*ista perfecta Saxonia*). So, less than two years after his accession, Æthelstan became king of a land 'which many kings had held separately before him'. Soon on his coinage and in his charters he would be 'Emperor of the whole world of Britannia': the most powerful ruler in these islands since the Romans.

Nothing was certain, however, and Æthelstan's England might have collapsed, but the creation of an allegiance under his successors is one of the great facts in early English history: loyalty to the king (or queen) and his or her law. This is why, in the twelfth century, Æthelstan was remembered as a kind of English Charlemagne – an image distantly echoed in several Middle English romances and even on the Elizabethan stage. The Victorians idealized him and his kinsmen in stained glass and storybooks, on Gilbert Scot façades, and on the friezes at Frogmore. For us now, he presents a very different image: the ferocity of his wars and feuds, of an empire held together by ceaseless itineraries, by the taking of hostages and tribute with enforced rituals of submission. Nonetheless, in a real sense, we still live in the state that has its origin in that moment in the tenth century.

* * *

So, as you can see, 'Turning Points' is a fascinating idea: constantly throwing up new insights, asking new questions, and perhaps pointing to how a new kind of British history curriculum might be taught in our schools. It is the tale of all our histories as Britons: the narrative of a nation of 'many races, languages, customs and clothes', as a tenth-century writer put it. Whatever our origin, as citizens of Britain, owing our allegiance to Her Majesty's government, it is the history of all of us.

1016

The Danish Conquest of England

SARAH FOOT

One eleventh-century date in English history is so well known to the general public that banks warn customers not to choose it as a PIN number. Yet that year, 1066, marked the fiftieth anniversary of another decisive battle that also led to the conquest of England, one that is now largely forgotten. On 18 October 1016, victory by a foreign force on a hilltop in Essex called Assandun brought this country within the sphere of an outside European power.

Just as the later Norman Conquest was to do, the Danish Conquest of 1016 threatened to alter the course of the island's history. Although ultimately short lived, it was unquestionably the most significant single event in the half-century from 1000 to 1049. Its repercussions continued after the native English royal line was restored in 1042 and it was still a factor in Harold Hardrada's first invasion and the ensuing battle of Stamford Bridge in that other momentous year, 1066. The victor in 1016 was the Danish king, Cnut (Canute), then a young man who had first come to England in 1013 with his father Swein Forkbeard. His opponent was similarly young and new to kingly power: Edmund, known as Ironside, son of Æthelred II, the infamously 'unready'.

Edmund did not die at Assandun, but the cream of the English army fell. In defeat Edmund was forced to make terms with Cnut and to divide England with him, retaining only Wessex for himself. How permanent such a division would prove was never tested, for Edmund died on 30 November of the same year and Cnut succeeded in persuading the English people to accept him as ruler of the entire kingdom. How did the realm that had so courageously defended itself against Viking attack in the ninth century, under King Alfred the Great, come to fall to that same enemy little more than a century later?

The conquest of 1016 was the culmination of years of intense warfare and latterly a concerted campaign. Swein had joined the force of Scandinavian chieftains, including Olaf Trygvasson, king of Norway, that attacked England in 994; he had led another prolonged campaign in 1003. In 1013 Swein was bent on conquest and his son, Cnut, participated in his father's military successes and saw him accepted as full king by all the English nation later that year.

With the English king, Æthelred, in exile among his wife's family in Normandy, this might have been the decisive moment of Danish conquest, bringing an end to years of warfare. Only the 'happy event' – in the words of the Abingdon chronicler – of Swein's death on 3 February 1014 gave Æthelred a second chance. While the Danish fleet elected Cnut as king, 'all the councillors who were in England', churchmen and laymen sent for Æthelred, telling him that 'no lord was dearer to them than their natural lord, if he would govern them more justly than he did before'. When Æthelred had made suitable promises, he came home to his people in the spring and was 'gladly received by them all'.

Whatever the extent of support for an English king in the south, the north was less loyal. The Anglo-Danish population of those regions where there had been substantial Scandinavian settlement during and after the First Viking Age were more ready to join Cnut. He made a base at Gainsborough in Lincolnshire, where he stayed until Easter. Before Cnut could attack Æthelred's forces in the south the king, capitalizing on the mood of enthusiasm that marked his return from exile, attacked first and drove Cnut out. Cnut set sail for Denmark, pausing only to leave at Sandwich the hostages given to his father, having first cut off their hands, ears and noses.

Again, this could have proved a decisive moment and the end of Danish hopes, but Æthelred's restoration failed to resolve his problems. He was ailing, his eldest son Æthelstan died in June 1014, and (reports are confused) there were tensions both with his surviving son Edmund and with the fickle ealdorman, Eadric Streona. Besides, with his record, Cnut would hardly abandon the fight for England. That his younger brother Harald had refused to share the kingdom of Denmark with him did nothing to weaken Cnut's resolve.

Cnut's campaign began at Sandwich in September 1015, from where he turned into Wessex and ravaged in Dorset, Wiltshire and Somerset. Meanwhile, divided English factions coalesced in two armies focused on Edmund Ironside and Ealdorman Eadric. Meeting Edmund but failing to fight, Eadric made a decision that was ultimately fatal to the English cause: he sided with Cnut, as did forty-five ships of Danish mercenaries, led by Thorkill the Tall. By Christmas 1015 the people of Wessex recognized the inevitable and accepted Cnut as their king, paying him and handing over hostages.

Now the situation of 1013 was reversed, for Edmund continued to hold the loyalty of at least parts of the north. During the Christmas feast of 1015, Cnut crossed the Thames into Mercia and started in early 1016 to maraud in Warwickshire. Edmund and Uhtred, earl of Northumbria, raised a force together and rampaged for their part in the north-west, especially in the lands of the traitorous Eadric. Cnut made for York, Uhtred's stronghold; Uhtred rushed there to defend his city but was forced to surrender and was later killed. With his own man, Erik, controlling Northumbria, Cnut was free to move southwards, pillaging as he went. He reached his ships by Easter (1 April) and turned on London, where Edmund had gone to join his sick father. When Æthelred died on 23 April 1016, the chief men in London elected Edmund as their king, but another group of magnates (according to one chronicler) elected Cnut and declared him king at Southampton.

More fighting ensued on several fronts as the Danes divided, some besieging London, others attacking Edmund, who had raised a force in Wessex. At this moment – when England's future lay in the balance – Eadric Streona changed sides again and went back to Edmund. Cnut used his fleet to cross the Thames to Essex and from there attacked Mercia (Eadric's stronghold). It was as he returned to his ships in October that Edmund overtook him and the two forces met at Assandun (identified either as Ashdon in the north-west of the county, or Ashingdon in south-east Essex). Following this resounding Danish victory, another battle came soon after, near the Forest of Dean (where Edmund's army was reinforced by Welsh troops). As winter approached, the two sides made peace. In addition to the division of England, Edmund agreed to the payment of a large tribute to Cnut's army. London, which had so long held out against the Danes, capitulated, paying tribute and offering winter quarters to

the Danes. Edmund's death on St Andrew's day sealed his
country's fate.

Victory in battle did not alone ensure Cnut's hold on
the English crown. Negotiations may have taken some
time and the payment of a huge tribute of £82,500 to
the Danes by an agreement reached at Oxford in 1018
probably marked the formal end of all hostilities. Cnut's
coronation in London by the archbishop of Canterbury
was an important symbolic act. The first coins Cnut issued
as king of the English show him wearing a crown, something that had not been depicted on the coinage since the
reign of Edgar in the tenth century.

The kingdom that Cnut had acquired was rich and
effectively organized. Although exhausted after years of
damaging warfare and recent political divisions, the population was anxious for peace and included prominent
men keen to follow a powerful leader. There was not, after
this conquest, the same removal of the native aristocracy
as followed the Norman invasion, but some important
English ealdormen were killed, including the treacherous
Eadric. While some of Cnut's followers received lands and
offices in England, many were rewarded with money and
returned to Denmark. Cnut divided his new realm into
four; he kept Wessex and the royal lands but gave East
Anglia to Earl Thorkill, Mercia to Ealdorman Eadric (before
his execution in 1017) and Northumbria to Earl Erik of
Hlathir. Although perhaps instituted as a military device,
to keep all the regions under tight control while the large
tribute payments were raised, the system of earldoms
remained throughout his reign. This enabled Cnut to levy
high levels of tax, in part to support his foreign ambitions
and in part to pay the mercenary troops who secured his
kingdom during his frequent absences.

Two law codes survive in Cnut's name, both drafted for
him by Wulfstan, archbishop of York, who had composed

law for King Æthelred. These are deeply religious in tone and reflect a king anxious to act justly and to protect and promote the interests of the Church. The reality experienced by the subjects of this often absentee king was far less benign than the image that Wulfstan portrays. Cnut's reign saw burdensome taxation and the maintenance of tight central control. For all his undoubted generosity to the Church, and his highly successful exploitation of England's efficient administrative machine (unparalleled in western Europe), Cnut's regime was the reverse of benevolent.

*　*　*

Cnut's conquest brought peace and prosperity, and gave England a more prominent role in Europe. The Danes' conquest of England in 1016 came not as a sudden event but as the result of years of intense fighting going back to the 980s when regular Viking attacks resumed for the first time since the days of Alfred the Great (871–99). It was the misfortune of Æthelred – whose epithet 'unready' relates to his lack of good counsel, not his unpreparedness – to rule England in such difficult circumstances. Although Æthelred's reputation has seen some scholarly rehabilitation in recent years, thanks particularly to Simon Keynes' re-evaluation of his methods of ruling, his popular image remains a negative one. Not least this is because we are dependent for a narrative of the wars on an account in the Anglo-Saxon Chronicle written after the Danish Conquest, which tends to see future failure in every temporary set-back.

For Æthelred's heirs, the conquest was a disaster. The æthelings (princes) Edward and Alfred were forced to spend their young adulthood in exile in Normandy. Their mother Emma had better fortune. She married Cnut in 1017, agreeing with her new husband that any sons of that marriage would have prior claim to England's throne over her older sons. Cnut's motives are not entirely clear. Did he marry her to make a gesture of continuity with the old regime? Or did he hope to prevent her and her brother Richard II, Duke of Normandy, from reinstating Æthelred's sons on the throne? Queen Emma was to play an active role in Cnut's government and participated also in his generosity to the Church; her half-Danish son ruled Denmark and England briefly after his father.

For the English, Cnut's conquest brought an end to years of warfare and initiated a period of peace and stability. More importantly, Cnut's rule brought England within a Scandinavian empire and gave the country, briefly, a place on wider European stages. Cnut was king of Denmark, Norway and part of Sweden; he also had authority of some sort over other parts of the British Isles. He married his daughter Gunnhild to the future German emperor Henry II and was present in Rome at the imperial coronation of Conrad II, Henry's father. A military leader of some prowess and a forceful but effective ruler, Cnut handled the conflicting demands of his widely spaced territory with firmness and skill. 'There had never', wrote Henry of Huntingdon in the 1120s, 'been a king of such greatness in England before.'

Henry of Huntingdon also reported the act for which Cnut is now best remembered. It was he who took his courtiers onto a beach and tried to prevent the advancing waves from wetting his feet. He did not do this from foolishness, or from arrogance, but to reveal the weakness of man in the face of the power of the Almighty. Together with his other acts of religious humility, this was part of Cnut's strategy to play down his bloody past and admit him, in Sir Frank Stenton's words, into the 'civilised fraternity of Christian kings'.

OTHER KEY DATES IN THIS PERIOD

1002 **Massacre of St Brice's Day** (13 November). King Æthelred ordered the killing of 'all the Danish men who were in England'. Often depicted as one of Æthelred's 'spasmodic acts of violence', this may be an exaggeration. Rather than massacre innocent Danish settlers in the Danelaw, he ordered the murder of mercenary Danes who had turned against their employers. After ten years of warfare, death and extortion, this was the people's revenge.

1012 **Institution of 'heregeld'** (army tax, later known as Danegeld), money paid to mercenary Danes. First paid on the dispersal in 1012 of the Viking force led by Thorkill the Tall that had plagued the country since 1009. Forty-five ships from the Danish army 'came over to the king [Æthelred], and they promised him to defend this country, and he was to feed and clothe them'.

1014 **Death of Swein Forkbeard**, election of Cnut, return of Æthelred from exile, after he had undertaken 'that he would be a gracious lord to them, and reform all the things which they all hated'. Æthelred came home to his people in the spring, 'and he was gladly received by them all'.

1020 **Cnut's generosity to the Church**. On the anniversary of his victory at Assandun, Cnut attended a ceremony for the consecration of a church at the battlesite as thanksgiving for the victory, and to honour the fallen. The monks of Bury St Edmund's Abbey claimed that it was in the same year that Cnut oversaw the replacement of secular clerics by Benedictine monks in their abbey and made them substantial gifts.

1028 **Cnut's conquest of Norway**. Cnut attacked Norway with ships and offered money to King Olaf's supporters to bribe them to his side. Olaf withdrew and in victory Cnut gave control of Norway to Earl Hakon, and, after his death, to his consort Ælfgifu of Northampton and their son

Swein. At the same time he gave authority in Denmark to his son Harthacnut by his wife Emma.

1031 **Submission of Scotland to Cnut**. Malcolm II, king of Scots 1005–34, had raided Northumbria in 1016, extending his border southwards. But in 1031 he had to submit to Cnut after the latter's campaign in the north, along with Macbeth, king of Moray, and another Scottish king. Evidence suggests that Cnut also had contact with the Irish and Welsh, perhaps being involved in a raid recorded in Wales in 1030.

1035 **Death of Cnut**. His two sons by different wives – Harold Harefoot and Harthacnut – each laid claim to his empire and to England. With Harthacnut in Denmark, Harold won the support of the English north of the Thames while Harthacnut's mother, Queen Emma, held Wessex for her son. Two years later, Harold was 'everywhere chosen as king', and Emma was exiled.

1040 **Death of Harold Harefoot**. Harthacnut promptly invaded England from Flanders with a fleet and took the throne. Chronicle reports of his rule are negative, accusing him of levying high taxes. He never married but was still young; if his health was poor, it might explain why he agreed to share the rulership with Edward before his sudden death while drinking at a marriage feast.

1042 **Accession of Edward the Confessor**. This brought an end to Danish power in England. Edward (Æthelred's son by Emma) came from exile in Normandy in 1041 to share rule with his half-brother, Harthacnut (Cnut's son by Emma). When Harthacnut died in 1042, Edward assumed kingship alone. He was crowned by the archbishops of York and Canterbury in Winchester Cathedral on Easter Day 1043. He ruled for a further twenty-three years and died in his bed. Childless, he failed to ensure a permanent restoration of the West Saxon dynasty, leaving the inheritance open to dispute, and a fresh invasion.

1066

William and the Normans arrive

NICHOLAS HIGHAM

In no other year in English history were four different men recognized as king by some part of the political community. 1066 was the last occasion on which a foreign invasion without substantial insular support toppled an English regime. Three great battles caused critical losses to the land-holding classes, then those who survived the last fight at Hastings faced dispossession. William, Duke of Normandy, presided over a cultural and social revolution: within a decade the upper echelons of society, both clerical and lay, were almost entirely foreign born; Old English had begun to be displaced as the language of elite discourse by French and Latin, and a wave of building, particularly of castles, new churches and monasteries, had begun to alter the landscape beyond recognition.

In the 1060s, England had for a generation been a comparatively peaceful kingdom under Edward the Confessor (1042–66). A handful of great earldoms connected local with national society; by the 1060s these were dominated by the Godwinesons, Edward's brothers-in-law (he was married to their sister, Edith) – Harold, Tostig, Gyrth and Leofwine – leaving only Mercia held by Edwin, grandson to Earl Leofric. However, Edward was clearly failing in midwinter 1065 and Westminster Abbey was hurriedly consecrated. 'Languishing from the sickness of soul', the king died on 4 January and was buried there the next day. The Bayeux Tapestry shows the old king, distinguished by his crown, shaggy hair and beard, as he extends his hand to his kneeling brother-in-law Harold. Edward's *Life*, written soon after, suggests that Edward commended 'this woman [the queen] and all the kingdom to your protection', and every version of the Anglo-Saxon Chronicle offers something similar. It seems likely, therefore, that Edward nominated Harold as his heir. In 1051/2, however, he had also apparently promised the succession to his maternal cousin, William of Normandy, but Edward's Norman friends had lost influence since and William had virtually no support in England.

Harold had the backing of every significant political group and of the English Church, and moved rapidly. He was crowned Harold II in Westminster Abbey on the same day that Edward was entombed. But he was not secure. Aside from William of Normandy, one or more Scandinavian claimants could be expected, as a result of the Danish occupation of the English throne from 1016 to 1042. Harald Hardrada of Norway had an awesome reputation and had already despatched a fleet to intervene in English politics in 1058, but his opponent, Swein of Denmark, had the better claim. Harold could also expect opposition from his brother Tostig, who in 1065 had, at Harold's instigation, been exiled from his earldom of Northumbria after a rebellion, and replaced by Edwin of Mercia's brother, Morcar. Harold's marriage to Edwin and Morcar's sister tied these two to his own candidacy at the price of excluding his brother.

On his accession Harold II was around 40, had a clutch of sons, had long been premier earl and was the only figure in England with a military reputation. He took control of the English administration, issuing coinage and sending out writs and charters. The combining of his own estates with those of the crown and Tostig made him far wealthier than his predecessor and there was no scope for opposition from England's Celtic neighbours or his own aristocracy.

Harold sent messengers to Normandy to inform William of Edward's death. The duke responded by claiming the throne and demanding that Harold honour his oath to support William's succession, which – according to Norman sources – Harold had made during a journey to the Continent around 1064. William then set about mobilizing forces and building a fleet. Additionally he conducted a diplomatic offensive, gaining the support of the pope and the emperor.

By late spring Harold had gathered substantial forces and was poised to withstand invasion. Halley's Comet appeared in late April 1066, and was perhaps interpreted as indicative of great events to come. William was delayed by the sheer scale of his preparations, so it was Harold's brother, Earl Tostig, who was the first outsider to appear. He had been at the court of Flanders and it was with a small Flemish fleet that he arrived off the Isle of Wight, recruiting men and raising supplies from his old estates. He then ravaged eastwards as far as Sandwich. Harold's departure from London with an army drove Tostig northwards, but he was again chased off by Edwin and Morcar. Tostig's Flemish forces abandoned him and he fled northwards to Malcolm, king of the Scots and an old ally.

Harold's forces remained ready throughout the summer but were stood down as the campaigning season waned, on 8 September. Harald Hardrada in Norway had, however, spent the summer raising a great host. His arrival was unexpected and he led a formidable force, estimated at three hundred vessels. Hardrada received Tostig's backing. His first objective was York, England's second city. Signs are that York closed its gates and awaited Mercian aid. Edwin and Morcar deployed their army outside the city but were defeated by the Norwegians on 20 September. York then had to surrender to Hardrada; it gave hostages and recognized him as king, and he withdrew eastwards to Stamford Bridge, to await the arrival of further hostages. On Monday 25th Harold advanced through York, reaching Stamford Bridge before news could reach Hardrada. The English army attacked and achieved complete victory. Hardrada and Tostig fell and their army was slaughtered. Stamford Bridge was one of the most decisive battles of the age, providing Harold with the kudos of a great warrior-king.

Across the Channel, William had been completing his preparations. Harold's departure from the south coast and then the arrival of suitable winds provided the duke with the opportunity to set sail about 26 September. His ships reached Pevensey on the 28th. The next day he moved his forces to Hastings, where he built a castle, and set about ravaging the Sussex coastal plain.

Harold marched south at speed, at the head of a substantial army. He perhaps hoped to surprise William but his enemies learned of his proximity and marched a short way inland. On Saturday 14 October, Harold deployed his infantry along the crest of a low hill – since occupied by Battle Abbey – confronting Norman attacks up the slope. The battle was long fought and the English army was routed only late in the day, but the outcome was determined by the deaths of Harold and his brothers, leaving the English cause leaderless.

William responded to victory cautiously, marching first

to Dover, which surrendered to him and was garrisoned. At London, the archbishops and surviving earls rallied behind the young Edgar the Ætheling (son of Edward the Confessor's half-nephew Edward the Exile), the only figure with an incontestable claim by descent. Although he is not known to have been crowned, Edgar was certainly active as king. However, he failed to mobilize a field army and could not stop the Normans firing Southwark. When William crossed the Thames at Wallingford, ravaging in an arc round London, the resolve of the English leadership melted away.

Despite a distinct lack of enthusiasm among the English, William's victory was viewed as so decisive an intervention by God that opposition could not be mobilized effectively. The Norman leader elected to be crowned at Westminster, where his relative, Edward the Confessor, lay buried, so reinforcing his claim. His acquisition of the crown marked a political revolution far more marked than Harold II's. While neither could claim royal descent, Harold was the candidate accepted by pretty much the entire English political class. William was an outsider; his victory came as leader of an army of foreign adventurers, whose lust for the rich estates of his new realm can only have alarmed the English. William must have found himself presiding over a mix of distrustful English magnates, whose language was incomprehensible to him, bishops who viewed him, however unwillingly, as God's anointed, and his own supporters, whose claims on his patronage would fuel a transfer of lands and resources rarely equalled in English history.

Norman conquest was not limited to the old Anglo-Saxon kingdom but pushed outwards into both Wales and Scotland within a generation. Following the battle of Mynydd Carn in 1081 the Earl of Chester overran much of North Wales while the Norman lords of Hereford and

Gloucester pushed into central and southern Wales. Even Rhys ap Tewdwr of Deheubarth accepted the overlordship of William and owed £40 per annum to the king at Domesday. In Scotland, Malcolm found himself similarly having to accept Norman overlordship, but it was not until his defeat and death that his sons oversaw the establishment of Norman barons in the Lowlands, including such famous names as Bruce and Balliol.

* * *

The England that William invaded was a stable and centralized state, but regional kingships or Viking influence remained in other parts of the British Isles. England was prosperous in the 1050s, with a growing population and expanding economy, but there were serious threats. Viking armies had displaced the English king Æthelred, bringing Danish kings to England between 1016 and 1042, and only wars in Scandinavia thereafter curtailed renewed invasion. Æthelred's son Edward was middle-aged when he came to the throne, and ageing by the 1050s. His marriage to Edith, Godwine's daughter, failed to produce an heir. The question of who should succeed was one of the most compelling political issues in Western Europe.

What sort of place was this England? It comprised arguably the most centralized state in Atlantic Europe. The court was well organized, with a rudimentary chancery; the monarchy was long established and strong, supported by estate revenues, land tax and profits from towns and industrial centres. Its coinage was regularly updated, with the head of the king displayed. The Church was well respected, with senior appointments managed by the crown. The administration was capable of raising large, well-equipped armies and naval forces. There were several major cities, such as London, Winchester and York, and around thirty smaller ones. Ships operating out of harbours scattered around the coasts from York to the West Country fished extensively and traded with the Continent, while Bristol and Chester shared the smaller Irish Sea trade. The majority of the population made their living from farming. Villages were coming into existence although many areas were still characterized by dispersed settlement. Manorial churches had become far more common over the previous century. Rural society operated within the structure of the shires, each with its fortified town that provided defences and markets and acted as centres for justice, taxation and ecclesiastical organization.

Ireland consisted of competing tribal kingships, with no urban centres, other than Viking Dublin and some Scandinavian-founded coastal sites, although there were major ecclesiastical centres, such as Armagh. Wales was divided between regional kingships, although Gruffudd ap Llywelyn (1039–63) had success in securing power in most of these, and had even constructed alliances in the English marches. Scotland had a single kingship, but regions of the north and west were under Scandinavian rule. Malcolm III (1058–93) exercised some influence in English affairs, both in terms of his relationships with a whole string of Northumbrian earls but also, following the Norman Conquest, via his marriage to Margaret, the sister of Edgar the Ætheling. Scotland, too, had virtually no urban development in this period and the kings were non-coin issuing.

OTHER KEY DATES IN THIS PERIOD

1051 **Godwine falls from favour.** King Edward and Earl Godwine, his father-in-law (and Harold's father), quarrelled over the royal appointment of a Norman as archbishop of Canterbury and the earl's refusal to punish the men of Dover for attacking Edward's French brother-in-law. A meeting at Gloucester led to confrontation and a second meeting at London, on 24 September, led to the flight of the old earl and his family abroad, most of them seeking aid in Flanders while Harold left for Ireland. Edward sent his wife Edith, Godwine's daughter, to a nunnery. Although it would be reversed the next year, the fall from power of Godwine's family seemed complete and Edward attempted to appoint his own men to exercise power under his kingship.

1054 **Macbeth is defeated.** Siward of Northumbria led an army into Scotland against Macbeth, defeating his forces and enthroning Malcolm III. Macbeth lived on for a few years but was eventually overthrown.

The death of Siward's eldest son and his nephew meant that when he died in 1055 there was no adult of his lineage to succeed, enabling the Godwinesons to secure Northumbria for Tostig.

1063 **Invasion of Wales.** Harold and Tostig took advantage of the youth of Mercia's new earl, Edwin, to invade Wales and destroy the power of his ally, King Gruffudd of Gwynedd and Powys. Harold sacked Gruffudd's halls at Rhuddlan, then in May led a fleet from Bristol against the Welsh coast, while Tostig invaded by land. The Welsh caved in and themselves killed Gruffudd in August; his ship's figurehead and trappings were delivered as trophies to King Edward, and Wales was placed by Harold in the hands of Gruffudd's half-brothers, who were forced to ally themselves with the victor, although they swiftly reverted to their family's alliance with Edwin of Mercia.

1068 **William faces opposition.** Opposition to King William's regime, its taxes and his patronage of foreigners was growing and he found it necessary to besiege Exeter, where Harold's mother was lodged.

Edgar the Ætheling took refuge in Scotland, where his sister Margaret was forced into marriage by King Malcolm. William appointed Robert of Commines as earl of Northumbria but he was overwhelmed at Durham on 28 January 1069, leading to a general rising of the north.

1072 Scotland acknowledges King William.

Having suppressed the northern rising (1069–70) and a revolt in the Fens (1071), William led a large force into Scotland. Malcolm III had given support to William's enemies and had allied himself with Edgar the Ætheling but could not withstand a full-blown Norman invasion. A meeting took place between the two kings, at which Malcolm was reported to have made his peace, given hostages – including his son Duncan – and acknowledged William's superiority.

1086 Domesday survey begins. Amid fears of Danish

invasion circulating in 1085, William recruited mercenaries in France to garrison the country. As the year began, his council set in motion the Domesday survey, sending out officials to build up a record of the estates of England, their occupiers and revenues, tax liability and other resources. The initial process was probably over by 1 August, when William met with his aristocracy at Salisbury and they took a new oath of allegiance before departing to fight the French.

1087 William's death. William was taken ill while on

campaign in France and died at the priory of St Gervais near Rouen on 9 September. He nominated his eldest son Robert to the duchy but it is unclear whether or not he named his second son, William Rufus, as king of England. However Rufus promptly left to secure this position and, aged about 27, he was crowned William II at Westminster later the same month.

1088 Odo's rebellion. Bishop Odo raised a rebellion

against his nephew, William II, and was joined by major figures who favoured Robert as king. The rebellion centred on Odo's castle of Rochester, which William besieged. The king rallied English support against his opponents, and his brother's efforts to reinforce the rebels failed. The affair ended with the departure of Odo overseas, leaving the new king in control.

1093

Fall of Malcolm. William II set about disposing of Malcolm of Scotland, whom he clearly viewed as over-mighty. Summoned to Gloucester, Malcolm was there refused admission to the king's presence and the treaty he desired. He returned home in anger, raised an army and made a rash attack on Northumbria but was trapped and killed. Malcolm was succeeded by his brother, Donald. Eventually Malcolm's daughter Matilda (or Maud) would marry Henry I, William I's youngest son, in 1100, capturing the English throne for her lineage.

1141

Stephen and Matilda fight a civil war

EDMUND KING

There had been three rulers of England in the year 1066, first Edward the Confessor, then Harold Godwineson and then William the Conqueror. So there would be in 1141 also, first Stephen, then Matilda and then Stephen (again). That Stephen would regain power was a result that no one would have expected after the battle that was fought at Lincoln on Candlemas Day, 2 February 1141.

On that day, outside the city walls, the Anglo-Norman lords, monitored by their kings, were a dynamic force. By 1135, they controlled most of the southern half of Wales, projecting their power from castles such as Cardiff, Brecon, Cardigan and Pembroke. The Scottish kings adapted to the same pattern, building castles and boroughs at centres such as Roxburgh, Berwick, Perth and Edinburgh, and Norman families such as the Bruces and Stewarts accepted their lordship.

The battle fought at Lincoln on 2 February 1141 seemed likely to prove no less significant than Assundun, if not Hastings. Outside the city walls, two substantial armies confronted each other. On the one side were King Stephen (*c.* 1092–1154, a grandson of William I, and Henry I's one-time protégé) with his earls – many created recently as a reward for loyalty – along with the baronage of northern England and troops from Flanders under William of Ypres. Opposing him, in the name of the Empress Matilda (1102–67, widow of Henry V of Germany, only legitimate daughter of Henry I) were her half-brother, Robert, earl of Gloucester, Ranulf, earl of Chester – whose ambition to control Lincoln had precipitated the battle – other magnates and 'a dreadful and unendurable mass of Welshmen'. It was a serious matter to fight an anointed king, and Stephen's side at first thought their opponents would engage in jousting and then retire; they were wrong.

King Stephen was very quickly abandoned by his 'false and factious earls'. He himself fought bravely, allegedly wielding a two-sided axe to good effect. But he was eventually captured. A voice rang out in the din of battle: 'Come here, everybody, come here: I've got the king!' This was William de Cahaignes, a vassal of the earl of Gloucester, and so indeed he had. Stephen surrendered to the earl and was taken to Gloucester, where he was 'presented' to the empress and then held in Bristol Castle.

The empress, though not present at Lincoln, was the main victor. She was her father's chosen successor; oaths to support her had been sworn to her more than once in his lifetime, by Stephen amongst others; and after she had come to England in September 1139 she had gained control over south-west England and the Welsh Marches, 'partly through fear, partly through respect' (as the chronicler William of Malmesbury put it). Now all was set fair for Matilda to gain the crown that had been promised to her and control over the whole of England. No wonder that she was reported to have been 'over the moon' when she first had news of King Stephen's capture.

The victory in battle needed legitimation. This was provided by a council of the English Church, which met at Winchester between 7 and 10 April 1141, under the presidency of Henry, bishop of Winchester (King Stephen's younger brother and the papal legate), and Theobald, archbishop of Canterbury. This body, after secret deliberations, 'elected' the empress as ruler, giving her the new title of Lady of England – an unprecedented title that allowed the magnates of England who had sworn allegiance to Stephen now to transfer their loyalty to the empress. It also allowed her to assume regalian authority. Matilda issued orders to the sheriffs of the counties and the barons of the exchequer; she referred to 'the pleas of my crown'; and she issued coins in her own name.

Yet from then on Matilda suffered a series of reverses. The first came in London. She could not claim a national authority unless she could establish a base in the capital. She was received by the Londoners around the middle of June, 'with magnificent processions'; but she knew she was not among friends and her behaviour cost her some of the friends that she had. Stephen and his family had a strong base in London and the home counties, particularly in Kent and Essex. The queen mustered troops on the south bank of the Thames at Southwark. Her brother-in-law the bishop of Winchester joined her in urging that while Stephen was in captivity the lands he had controlled before he became king should be granted to his son, Eustace. 'The empress would not hear of it,' and her caution is understandable, but her refusal allowed her enemies to claim that other magnates would be treated in the same way and were liable to lose their lands. All the news from London brought tales of Matilda's arrogance and insensitivity. She was losing the propaganda war.

While all this was happening in the corridors and the cloisters of power, in the streets of London there was turmoil. Lincoln had been sacked after the battle, and a reputation for hostility to mercantile ambition preceded the empress into the city. On 24 June, taking advantage of the cover of the midsummer revels, the townspeople swarmed out of the city gates, 'like bees from a hive', and made for Matilda's lodgings at Westminster. She was 'reclining at a well-cooked feast', so it was reported, when she had news of their approach and was forced to flee in disarray.

Worse was to follow. After a meeting at Oxford in late July, she returned to Winchester. There she hoped to establish what she could claim to be a national base. In the course of five weeks' fighting, though, Winchester also became too hot for her. She was in danger of being entrapped in the castle to the west of the city when she broke cover and escaped. She managed to reach Devizes in Wiltshire, 'quite terrified', slung across her horse 'like a corpse'. Her brother, Robert of Gloucester, however, was captured by Stephen's forces at Stockbridge Ford in Hampshire.

There were then discussions aimed at securing a permanent peace but all that could be agreed was that the king and the earl be exchanged for one another, 'no other conditions being involved', and that 'they should return to the earlier position in the civil war'. The exchange took place on 1 November. It remained for a further Church council to restore Stephen to the throne and for him then to be recrowned at Canterbury on Christmas Day. This was more than a simple crown-wearing: King Stephen had been sullied by his captivity and the job needed to be done again. When Richard I was released from captivity and recrowned in 1194 the monks of Canterbury turned up the same order of service that they had used in 1141.

Stephen was king at the end of 1141, just as he had been at the beginning. This hardly seems to indicate a 'turning point' in English history. What made it so was not the events of the year but the reaction to them, in particular to the fact that king and empress resumed their hostility as though nothing had happened. 'These indeed were harsh and ill-judged terms and bound to do harm to the entire country,' wrote the London-based author of the *Gesta Stephani*. William of Malmesbury said that the year was 'ill-omened and almost mortal to England'. The political commentators spoke with one voice and they spoke for the nation. The year 1141 had been one that had brought the whole political process into disrepute.

Over the next decade the lessons of 1141 would be learned. The churchmen had not listened to the lay magnates and had given Matilda the crown without insisting on a peace settlement. Henry of Winchester had been peremptory when caution was called for. Matilda had been imperious when conciliation was called for. She wished to rule in her own right but this was not acceptable to the English in 1141 any more than it had been in 1135.

The focus would now be on her son, 'Henry, the son of the daughter of King Henry, the rightful heir of England and Normandy' (the title that he gives himself in a charter of 1141). In 1153, with the clergy and the magnates acting together and mandating a peace process, this claim was accepted and in 1154, on Stephen's death, he became Henry II, king of England. It would be a victory for statesmanship, a quality that had been lacking in 1141. Henry was carefully presented to the English not as an Angevin ruler but as a king in the line of the English succession that stretched back before the conquest of 1066. John of Salisbury, in his *Policraticus*, would insist that the new king 'principally relied on fellow countrymen'; it was Stephen who was now represented as a 'foreigner'.

The final lesson of 1141 was that the crown of England was not a commodity but a trust, and that all of the nation were trustees. It is that realization that makes the year a turning point in English, and later British, history.

* * *

With this in mind, it is important to note that England was a wealthy country in the first half of the twelfth century, and its economy grew rapidly. It grew because new lands were taken in from the forest and the fen, and because the scale of the market grew. The east coast ports mushroomed – some of them, such as Grimsby and Boston, had not even been mentioned in Domesday Book. Enterprising landowners, their rent rolls fixed, sought to make a profit from trade. The great fairs of England, such as Winchester, which had grown to sixteen days by 1155, were money-spinners for their lords. The upland areas of the British Isles grew more slowly, though there were significant mineral deposits, including the silver mines of Carlisle, the profits of which went to the Scots during Stephen's reign.

In important respects, the ethos of the ruling class changed from one based on consumption to one based on profit. The professionalization of royal financial management was exemplified in the exchequer. The sheriffs accounted at Winchester twice a year, their returns collected in the first royal accounts, the 'pipe rolls', one of which survives for 1129–30. Another facet of the new professionalism was the growth of the Cistercian order. The monks were given partly cleared lands by their patrons; and their manors and granges were managed for profit.

After 1106, Henry I, the Conqueror's youngest and most able son, ruled both England and Normandy. 'He always attempted to give peace to his subject peoples', said Orderic Vitalis, 'and strictly punished law-breakers.' He projected his authority beyond his frontiers. In 1114, 'the Welsh princes came to him and became his vassals'. In 1119, the French king, Louis VI, was defeated in battle at Brémule. Henry's brother-in-law, David of Scots (king of Scots, 1124–53), and his nephews, Theobald, Count of

Blois, and Stephen, Count of Mortain (king of England, 1135–54), attended his court.

In the second quarter of the century what was becoming a family firm suffered a managerial crisis. The underlying cause was the uncertainty about, followed by a dispute over, the succession. Henry's only legitimate son William, all were agreed, 'would have obtained the kingdom as of right'. But he died in 1120 and Henry's second marriage proved barren. The oaths that were sworn to his daughter, the Empress Matilda, for the first time on 1 January 1127 proved inadequate to secure her succession when Henry died, and served to weaken the new king, Stephen. There followed what the Anglo-Saxon Chronicle described as 'nineteen long winters', during which 'Christ and his saints were asleep'.

Stephen made a series of concessions by which the imperium of Henry I shrank to something close to a provincial lordship. In 1136, Stephen ceded Carlisle to David, king of Scots, and subsequently he granted his son, Henry, the earldom of Northumbria. With civil war occupying English interests in the 1140s, the prospect of Scotland holding onto Northumbria was not out of the question, though in 1152 the early death of King David's son Henry weakened Scottish power.

In 1136 also the Welsh gained a number of victories over the Norman settlers, and in 1139 the empress landed and established control over the West Country.

The battle of Lincoln was of short-term significance in England, but it led inexorably to the king's losing control over Normandy. The take-over of the duchy by the empress's husband, Geoffrey, Count of Anjou, completed in 1144, drew upon the lessons of what had happened in England in 1141, with the securing of a political consensus, and a leading role being taken by the citizens of Rouen, who were growing rich from trade along the Seine.

OTHER KEY DATES IN THIS PERIOD

1100 **Marriage of Henry I.** When William Rufus was killed hunting in the New Forest on 2 August, his younger brother, Henry, moved swiftly, being crowned at Westminster just three days later. He married Matilda (Maud, also known as Edith), daughter of Malcolm Canmore, king of Scots, and Margaret, daughter of Edward the Ætheling, later in the year. Their children would thus claim descent both from the Norman and the Anglo-Saxon kings of England.

1110 **Betrothal of Henry's daughter.** Matilda's marriage to the German emperor, Henry V, was secured at the cost of a huge dowry of 10,000 marks, raised by a special geld taken at three shillings on the hide. The couple were married in 1114, when Matilda was not quite 12, but she was widowed in 1125. There were no children of this marriage.

1120 **Wreck of the *White Ship*.** The court returned from Barfleur to England on 25 November. One of the boats, the *White Ship*, ran aground on rocks close to the shore. Henry's only legitimate son, William Ætheling (aged 17), was lost, along with two of the king's illegitimate children and many of the nobility. The king's plans for a peaceful succession went down with the ship.

1124 **Accession of King David I of Scotland.** The Scottish king succeeded Alexander I to the throne. He is credited with moving Scottish society more towards the Anglo-Norman model and extending the reach of royal authority. A strong and capable king, he took advantage of the turmoil in England to expand his realm into Northumbria.

1132 **Foundation of Rievaulx Abbey.** The spread of the Cistercian order, the 'white monks', was a particular feature of the first half of the twelfth century. Rievaulx in North Yorkshire would become the largest of these monasteries, growing under its superior, St Ailred (abbot 1147–67), to a community of 140 choir monks and 500 lay brothers.

1135 **Death of Henry I of England.** The king died during the night of 1 December at the hunting lodge of Lyons-la-Forêt, near Rouen, having – according to Henry of Huntingdon – disobeyed his doctors and eaten a dish of lampreys, a fish delicacy. He was buried at Reading Abbey, which he had founded, on 5 January 1136, in the presence of his successor, Stephen, an outcome that would have disappointed but not surprised him.

1138 **Battle of the Standard.** A Scottish army, invading in support of the empress, was stopped and defeated soon after it crossed the river Tees (the point at which a raid became an invasion in English eyes). The northern baronage and local militias, mustered by Thurstan, archbishop of York, fought under the banners of their saints: these were stacked up to form a 'standard', which gave the battle its name.

1147 **The Second Crusade.** The English played a significant though a supportive role in the crusade – preached by St Bernard – whose armies set out in the spring of 1147. British forces shared in the capture of Lisbon but shared also in failure in the Holy Land. The wealthy William, third earl of Surrey (earl de Warenne) was killed in the defiles of Laodicea.

1149 **Knighting of Henry fitz Empress.** Henry (1133–89), the eldest of Empress Matilda's sons, was knighted at the age of 16 on Whitsunday at Carlisle by his uncle, David, king of Scots. This marked the beginning of the future Henry II's adult career. When he returned to Normandy, his father, Geoffrey Plantagenet, Count of Anjou (whom Matilda had married in 1128 – he was 11 years her junior), invested him with the duchy, as being his by right of inheritance.

1171

Henry II invades Ireland

JOHN GILLINGHAM

On 17 October 1171 an armada of four hundred ships put in at Crook on the south coast of Ireland. That day, for the first time ever, a king of England set foot on Irish soil. Henry II landed in force, intending to make the Irish recognize him as their overlord. He stayed six months, long enough to change the course of Irish history. Writing only twenty-five years later a Yorkshire historian, William of Newburgh, in a chapter that he entitled 'The Conquest of the Irish by the English', summed up the impact of Henry II's expedition thus: 'a people who had been free since time immemorial, unconquered even by the Romans, a people for whom liberty seemed an inborn right, were now fallen into the power of the king of England.'

Not surprisingly, the whole episode has given rise to fierce controversy. Was it, as Irish nationalist tradition held, an invasion by a malevolent English king? Or had Henry II gone to Ireland, as the late Victorian historian J.H. Round put it in 1899, 'because her people were engaged in cutting one another's throats; we are there now because, if we left, they would all be breaking one another's heads'. Or had he been reluctantly drawn in because he needed to retain control over his own most turbulent subjects – a number of lords of the Welsh Marches who were on the point of carving out independent territories for themselves in Ireland? One English chronicler reported that the Irish themselves asked him to come to their help against the most powerful of those lords, Richard de Clare, later known as Strongbow.

Three things are certain. The first is that 1171 had begun disastrously for King Henry II. He was at Argentan in Normandy when a New Year present reached him in the shape of the news that as darkness fell on 29 December 1170 four of his knights had killed the archbishop of Canterbury. Stunned by the knowledge that his own angry words had precipitated the murder of his one-time friend, for three days Henry refused to eat anything or talk to anyone. Whether genuine or feigned, this display of grief reveals Henry's awareness of the damage done to his reputation by the widely held assumption that the killers had acted on his orders. During the following months he sought to save his honour, even offering to submit to the judgement of Pope Alexander III and, if need be, in person. It soon became clear that one of the cleverest moves he could make was to play the Irish card. By going to Ireland he could both create a cooling-off period and pose as the Church's champion, bringing ecclesiastical and moral reform to a backward province.

The second certainty is that the logistical preparations for Henry's expedition were massive. Supplies for the fleet arrived from all over England, including enormous quantities of food for the troops, and luxuries such as silks and no less than 569 pounds of almonds for Henry and his courtiers. Gloucestershire alone sent five carts, four wagons, 3,000 spades, 2,000 pickaxes and 60,000 nails, while Winchester provided 1,000 pounds of wax for candles and to seal documents. Economic development in England meant that its king disposed of military hardware – ammunition, armour and castles – on a scale that none of his Celtic neighbours could match. As a consequence, Henry II approached the conquest of Ireland with confidence.

The third certainty is that Henry's preferred solution to the problems posed by men such as Strongbow was to take the whole of Ireland into his lordship, irrespective of the views of the Irish themselves. After all, the Irish, in Henry's eyes, were both thoroughly uncivilized and in no position to make their opinions count. In truth, Ireland in 1171 was a deeply divided society. Learned Irish scholars taught that their land was divided into two halves, northern and southern; into five provinces – Leinster, Munster, Ulster, Connacht and Meath; and into more than a hundred peoples (*tuatha*), each one ruled over by a chief (*toisech*) or by a king (*rí*). A mini-kingdom with a radius of ten miles was by no means impossibly small. Each *rí túaithe* owed tribute and military service to more powerful neighbouring kings. They in turn owed allegiance to kings who were, or claimed to be, supreme in one of the provinces. When a powerful king died, a struggle for kingship within the family ensued while more established kings in other kingdoms took full advantage. In this state of flux scores of kings competed to be the strongest in a province, or even to be the greatest king in all Ireland, sometimes known as *rí Erenn*, king of Ireland, or the 'high king'. The competition for resources and prestige took the form of war, of cattle raid and counter-raid, in which casualties were often high.

In one of these struggles for power, in 1166, Diarmait, king of Leinster, had been driven out of Ireland. With Henry II's permission, he recruited a small band of soldiers and managed to regain a foothold in his family's homeland in south Leinster. In 1169 and 1170 more mercenaries crossed the Irish Sea, lured by Diarmait's promises of land

and money. To Richard de Clare, Diarmait promised the hand of his daughter Aífe and, in flagrant breach of Irish custom, the succession to Leinster. In August and September 1170 Diarmait and Strongbow won some striking successes, capturing the two biggest towns in Ireland: Waterford and Dublin. When Diarmait died in the spring of 1171, Strongbow became *de facto* king of Leinster. It was at this point that Henry II decided to intervene. Strongbow travelled to England to come to terms with Henry and to do homage to him for Leinster. But the king of England had no intention of calling off his invasion plans.

On 18 October Henry entered Waterford, and there began the process of taking the submissions of Irish kings. Some of the 'modernizers' among Irish ecclesiastics welcomed the king of England as an ally in their attempts to reform the Irish Church. Letters from them led Alexander III to express his joy at the news that 'a barbarous and uncivilised people has been made subject to the noble king of the English.' Henry assumed the title 'Lord of Ireland' – which was retained by all subsequent kings of England until 1541, when another bruiser, Henry VIII, decided it would be nicer to be called king of Ireland too.

In November Henry II went to Dublin, where he had a new 'Irish-style' palace built. Here he celebrated Christmas 1171, holding court and trying to impress the invited Irish with a demonstration of nouvelle cuisine. By now many Irish kings had submitted; but not all. The high king, Ruaidrí Ua Conchobair (Rory O'Connor), king of Connacht, kept his distance. According to one of Henry's clerks, despite the wet weather and the mountainous and boggy terrain, it would have been easy to defeat O'Connor, had not other urgent business meant that the king had to leave Ireland in a hurry in April 1172. That business was the arrival of papal legates in Normandy, who had come north, Henry had been informed, to settle the question of his responsibility for the murder of Thomas Becket.

Before Henry II left, however, he confirmed the conquests that the newcomers had already made. His decision to have Dublin, Wexford and Waterford administered by royal officials meant that the English crown kept the richest prizes for itself. When Laurence O'Toole, the last Irish archbishop of Dublin, died, he was replaced by John Comyn, one of Henry II's chancery clerks.

Despite Henry's burgeoning influence, most of the island remained in the hands of Irish kings. In 1175 Henry recognized O'Connor as their overlord in return for O'Connor's recognition of him as his overlord and a payment of tribute measured in cattle hides. But this agreement – the Treaty of Windsor – soon lapsed. Nothing stopped Henry II and his successors from granting as yet unconquered Irish kingdoms to English favourites. As a result, Ireland remained, as it had always been, a land of war, no longer just between Irish and Irish, but often now between Irish and English.

For a hundred years or so Ireland remained a land of opportunity, and while Britain's population continued to grow, thousands were willing to emigrate. By founding towns and villages, building mills and bridges, these colonists almost turned south and east Ireland into another England overseas. In King John's reign, the 'Anglicization' of Ireland was made official government policy. But when the movement of settlers ran out of steam, in around 1300, a Gaelic resurgence drove the English back behind the Pale (the fortified area around Dublin). Not for many centuries would it be possible to say that the conquest of Ireland started by Henry II had been completed. Irish tradition identified 1169 as 'the year of destiny', but it was by going there in 1171 and leaving again in 1172 that Henry II set a pattern for that catastrophic mixture of force and neglect that was to characterize the English government's treatment of the Irish for centuries to come.

* * *

It had been the rebranding of Ireland as the 'island of barbarians' that gave Henry his opportunity to strike: Henry II was certainly not the first king of England to turn his eyes towards Ireland.

The first two Norman kings, William the Conqueror and William II, William Rufus, were rumoured to have contemplated taking it over, the latter allegedly toying with the idea of building a bridge of boats from Wales. Henry II himself thought about it as early as 1155, perhaps at the request of the Church. The archbishops of Canterbury had been claiming to be primates of the whole of Britain and Ireland since the 1070s, but this claim took a severe blow in 1152 when a papal legate restructured the Irish Church with no reference to Canterbury whatsoever. It may have been as a result of lobbying from Canterbury that Adrian IV, still the only Englishman to have ever become pope, sent Henry II a letter giving him Ireland. But in 1155 other matters intervened and Henry dropped the idea – supposedly on his mother's advice.

Although Adrian's readiness to grant Ireland to the king of England has often been regarded as just the kind of thing an English pope would do, it probably reflected his zeal for church reform much more than his Englishness. He shared the view of the French Cistercian abbot, Bernard of Clairvaux, the most influential European churchman of his generation, who described the Irish as: 'shameless in their customs, uncivilised in their ways, godless in religion, barbarous in their law, obstinate as regards instruction, foul in their lives, Christians in name, pagans in fact'.

By the time Henry II came to the throne, profound economic and social changes in much of Europe, including England, had led to those regions in which little had as yet changed being seen in a new and highly critical light. The Scots and the Welsh found themselves tarred by the same brush, but it was the Irish who suffered most. According to William of Malmesbury, 'whereas the English and French live in market-oriented towns and enjoy a cultivated style of life, the Irish live in rural squalor.' The acceptance of new laws of marriage in most of Europe – when in Ireland divorce and remarriage continued to be lawful – led to Anselm of Canterbury accusing the Irish of swapping wives 'in the same way that other men exchange horses'. Ireland, formerly thought of as 'the island of saints', was being rebranded as the 'island of barbarians'. It was the pope's duty, as he saw it, to bring the Irish to a better way of life, a truer Christianity, and if that meant invasion and regime change, then so be it. This was the atmosphere in which Henry II calculated that even he could present himself as a good son of the Church.

As early as the tenth century, kings of England had liked grandiloquent titles such as 'king of the English and of all other peoples living in the ambit of the British island'. But until 1171 these had remained just empty words. Now they had been given a new kind of reality – and this just when those peoples whose lands were being invaded had been stereotyped as immoral and primitive savages.

OTHER KEY DATES IN THIS PERIOD

1152 **Henry's marriage to Eleanor of Aquitaine.** The divorce of French King Louis VII and the 30-year-old duchess of Aquitaine in March was followed, just eight weeks later, by her marriage to the most ambitious young ruler in France, the 19-year-old Henry, Duke of Normandy and Count of Anjou. This marked the beginning of the Plantagenet connection with Bordeaux – and its wine trade – that was to last for the next three hundred years. Henry was now set to rule greater dominions than any previous king of England.

1153 **Angevin invasion of England.** In January, despite the threats from enemies jealous of his recent good fortune, Duke Henry dared to sail to England to claim the kingdom that had belonged to his grandfather, Henry I. By August he had still made little progress when the unexpected death of King Stephen's eldest son Eustace so disheartened the old king that he came to terms with Henry, recognizing him as his heir in return for his own life possession of the throne and a guarantee that his second son, William, could keep the family estate.

1166 **Creation of a public prosecution service.** Henry II ordered sheriffs to empanel juries whose job it was to name those whom they suspected of serious crime. The sheriff was to bring suspects to trial before the king's judges when they visited the shire. Those found guilty were punished by the 'crown'. This legislation – the Assize of Clarendon – helped establish Henry's reputation as a founder of the common law.

1173 **Queen Eleanor's rebellion.** The greatest threat to Henry II came from his own wife when she led their three eldest sons, Henry, Richard and Geoffrey, into revolt and into alliance with kings William of Scotland and Louis VII of France (her own ex-husband). After Henry's eventual victory (summer 1174), he was reconciled with his sons, but Eleanor was kept a prisoner until he died. Her rebellion had challenged the authority of husbands everywhere.

1174 **Canterbury and Scotland.** On 12 July Henry II was flogged by the monks of Canterbury Cathedral, his public penance for his involvement in the murder of Thomas Becket. The dead saint (Becket had been canonized in 1173) quickly accepted his apology. On 13 July Henry's great enemy, King William of Scotland, was captured while leading an invasion of England. William was forced to accept the Treaty of Falaise (8 December), by which Scotland was subject to the king of England, whose troops now occupied Edinburgh, Berwick and Roxburgh.

1176 **The first Eisteddfod.** Rhys ap Gruffudd of Deheubarth held what a Welsh chronicle called 'a special feast at Cardigan, and he set two kinds of contests: one between the bards and the poets, and another between the harpists, pipers and players of other instruments. He set two chairs for the victors . . . and rewarded them with great prizes.'

1187 **Fall of Jerusalem.** Saladin's capture of Jerusalem on 2 October, the anniversary of Muhammad's night journey into heaven from the holy city, shocked the Christian world. The kings of England, France and Germany vowed to go on crusade and, to fund the expedition, Henry II imposed a tax called the Saladin tithe, but died before departing. It was left to his son, Richard I, to lead the Third Crusade.

1189 **Restoration of Scottish independence.** After his father's death in 1189, Richard I decided that it was time to make peace with King William of Scotland. In December he restored both castles and Scottish independence in return for a hefty sum. In the words of the earliest Scottish historian, John of Fordun, Richard was 'that noble king so friendly to the Scots'. When Richard was later held prisoner in Germany, King William even contributed to his ransom.

1199 **A reforming chancellor?** John was crowned king of England on 27 May, and on the same day Hubert Walter, archbishop of Canterbury, formerly Richard I's most trusted minister, was appointed chancellor. As a result of his work as director of the royal secretariat, the first year of the new king's reign saw an explosive proliferation of government records. This was to persuade many twentieth-century historians that John must have been an unusually business-like king.

1215

Magna Carta is forced on John

DAVID CARPENTER

The year of Magna Carta, 1215, when an English ruler was first subjected to the law, has resonated down the ages as a landmark in Britain's constitutional history. Indeed, in *BBC History Magazine*'s 2006 poll, its anniversary was voted the most suitable date on which the nation should celebrate Britishness. The charter itself still lives. Its most fundamental chapters remain on the statute book of the UK as barriers to arbitrary rule. They condemn the denial, sale and delay of justice, and forbid imprisonment and dispossession save by lawful judgement of one's peers (social equals), or the law of the land.

The charter was negotiated at Runnymede between 10 and 15 June 1215, with King John riding down each day from Windsor, and the barons encamped in their tents across the meadows beside the Thames. On 15 June, John, tricky to the end, refused more concessions and simply sealed the charter – 'take it or leave it' – thereby cleverly keeping the names of the twenty-five barons who were to enforce its terms out of the document, this because they had still to be chosen. John hoped the charter would become no more than a toothless symbol of his generosity to the kingdom; the barons hoped that its terms would be rigorously enforced and indeed extended. The result was civil war.

By September, John had got the pope to quash the charter. That month, the opposition barons deposed John and offered the throne to Louis, eldest son of King Philip II of France. He came to England in May 1216 and by the time of John's death in October controlled more than half the kingdom. In the north Alexander II of Scotland had gained Carlisle, and was making good his claims to Cumberland, Westmorland and Northumberland. In Wales, Llywelyn ap Iorwerth, ruler of Gwynedd, had swept through the south and taken the royal bases of Cardigan and Carmarthen.

Yet John's dynasty survived, and with it, paradoxically, the charter. Its implantation into English political life was the work of the minority government of John's son, Henry III, who was only 9 on his accession. Magna Carta was also a British document. Both Alexander and Llywelyn had been with the rebels from the start, and both benefited from the charter's terms, terms that acknowledged 'the law of Wales' and invoked for the Welsh, as for Alexander, the principle of judgement by peers. Ultimately, as Wales and Scotland became part of a United Kingdom, their peoples too were embraced by the charter's protections. The charter, however, was no panacea. Since the clause setting up the twenty-five barons was left out from post-1215 versions of the document, it had no constitutional means of enforcement. It also said nothing about how the king's ministers were to be chosen, patronage distributed and policy decided, major holes that defined the political battleground of the later middle ages.

The charter made a profound difference. It clamped down on various sources of revenue. Henceforth the 'relief' or inheritance tax paid by an earl or baron was to be £100, not the thousands of pounds sometimes demanded by John. It facilitated the spread of the common law and made justice less open to bargaining or bribery. It gave the gentry concessions they could exploit to make the running of local government more acceptable. Above all it asserted a fundamental principle: the king was subject to the law, the law that Magna Carta had made. As a result, arbitrary rule became more difficult and resistance to it more legitimate.

In 1214 John's long-planned campaign to recover his continental empire had ended in disaster with his allies decisively defeated at Bouvines. John returned to England a sitting duck, his treasure spent. Suspicious and untrustworthy, a womanizer and a murderer, he was loathed by many of his barons. His huge financial exactions over several years had antagonized the wider political community. By early 1215 a large group of barons, many from the north, where his rule had seemed particularly severe, were in league, and were demanding reform. They were abetted by Scotland's King Alexander and Llywelyn of Wales.

John played for time and summoned a council to meet at Oxford towards the end of April. Instead the barons met in arms at Stamford in Lincolnshire, from where on 5 May they renounced their allegiance to the king, the beginning of civil war. The war was transformed within a fortnight by the Londoners letting the baronial rebels into the city – its walls and wealth protected the baronial cause, and made any quick royalist victory impossible. Yet baronial victory too could not be quick. John retained his castles, many commanded by ruthless military experts. Shrewd use of patronage meant he also retained the loyalty of some of the greatest barons. So the result towards the end of May was a truce and the start of the negotiations that ended with the charter at Runnymede.

The charter was the product of the way John and his predecessors has ruled since the Norman Conquest. It also reflected the nature of early thirteenth-century English society, in part through its omissions. Take the place of women in the charter: they certainly appeared, for important clauses secured for baronial widows their dowers and inheritances and protected them from being forced into remarriage by the king. The clause reflected that baronial women did have property rights: they could inherit land; they received as dower a portion (usually a third) of their husband's lands on his death. The clause had a real effect and the thirteenth century was graced by large numbers of baronesses who spent years as widows controlling extensive lands.

Yet the charter did nothing to alter the inequalities between men and women. Women only inherited if they had no brothers. They virtually never held office, and, for all their influence behind the scenes, played virtually no public part in politics. No women featured in the list of those who had counselled John to concede the charter. The clauses in the charter itself were designed not to liberate women, but to protect their male children from having their mother's property carried off by second husbands.

Even less privileged were the peasants. They made up perhaps 75 per cent of the population, half of them 'villeins', which meant they were legally unfree. Peasants featured in Magna Carta – the stipulation that sheriffs should not force men and villages to work on bridges dealt specifically with their predicament. So did the clause which laid down that fines imposed on villeins were to be reasonable and assessed by men of their neighbourhood. To no one, John promised in one of the most famous clauses, would he sell, deny or delay justice. But there lay the rub, for it was the law itself that made half of the peasantry unfree, leaving them excluded from the king's courts and at their lord's mercy in anything concerning the terms on which they held their lands. The charter did nothing to alter this. Indeed, the protection it did afford peasants was exclusively against the oppressions of royal agents. They were protected from the king so that they could be exploited all the better by their lords.

Against its meagre concern for women and peasants, the charter catered abundantly for the great players. It gave freedom to the Church (which held over a quarter of England's land), and reiterated John's promise that bishops and abbots could be elected free from royal interference, thus dealing with a major grievance. The Church was to play a key part in publicizing John's charter and in supporting the later versions made by Henry III. London, as we have seen, was the great baronial base. Its population early in the thirteenth century was perhaps as high as 40,000, making it Britain's largest city. The charter protected the privileges of all the kingdom's cities and boroughs but London's alone were mentioned by name, and it received an additional promise that it should be free from arbitrary taxation.

Most striking of all was the charter's treatment of the knights. In the 1200s there were about 5,000 of them in England's counties, the backbone of local government. One contemporary chronicler, Ralph of Coggeshall, averred that all the barons who remained loyal to John were deserted by their knights; an exaggeration, but it shows the flow of the tide. The charter laid down that the king's judges hearing assizes in the counties were to sit with four knights of each county, elected in the county court, a testimony both to the self-confidence of the knights and their determination to control the workings of justice in the localities. Another clause empowered twelve knights in each county, again elected in the county court, to investigate and abolish the evil practices of the king's local officials. The zeal with which the knights went about their work was a major factor in John's decision to abandon the charter.

Above all, the charter met the grievances of the earls and barons. There were around a dozen earls in the early thirteenth century, and something between one hundred and two hundred barons. Tiny numbers, but they controlled a large part of the country's wealth, and had mostly been in rebellion. Not surprisingly, they stamped their mark on the charter's early clauses, making it very much a baronial document. Thus Chapter 2, as we have seen, fixed the relief of earls and barons at £100. Chapter 4 protected baronial lands from exploitation by the king when they were in his hands during the minority of an heir. Chapter 14 vested the power to consent to taxation in the hands of a largely baronial assembly. Indeed, only the greater barons, lay and ecclesiastical, were to receive individual letters of summons to it. The implication was that the earls and barons, commanding the allegiances of their tenants, could answer for the realm.

The charter thus reflected the structures of power in English society. It was also the product of ideas. The king should govern lawfully for the good of his people. He should only punish individuals after having obtained a judgement of their peers. A king who defied these principles could be regarded as a tyrant, and might be restrained or even deposed. By 1215 such concepts had a long pedigree and were commonplace among John's opponents. They were sharpened and refined by the archbishop of Canterbury, Stephen Langton, an internationally famous academic, who played a key role in brokering the 1215 settlement, and in supporting the charter thereafter. It was these ideas, enshrined in the charter, that formed its essential legacy, a legacy first for England, and ultimately for the United Kingdom as a whole.

* * *

Britain in the age of Magna Carta was full of contrasts, with profound differences in social structure between the uplands of Wales and Scotland and lowland England. Hence the way the English, living in nucleated villages and eating bread – product of their great corn-growing fields – could stigmatize the Scots as bare-buttocked Highlanders and ridicule the Welsh as dwellers in dispersed settlements, who consumed nothing but milk and meat.

Yet, in many ways, the peoples of Britain were becoming more alike. The structure of dioceses and parishes, and the houses of Benedictine and Cistercian monks, had spread through the island. The Scottish nobility had been transformed in the twelfth century by the king's establishment of Anglo-Norman aristocrats, men of chivalric outlook. The castles, cavalry, armour, seals and documents of the Welsh rulers show how they had been influenced by their Anglo-Norman neighbours. Royal government in Scotland, however, was comparatively decentralized. Wales was divided between competing princes. Only in England was the power of the ruler so insistent and intrusive as to provoke demands for restraints.

The grievances dealt with in Magna Carta had a long history. Many were the product of the way kings since the Norman Conquest had manipulated the judicial process and exploited the rights and revenues that came to them from the new tenurial structures introduced by the Norman Conquest. Already in 1100 Henry I's Coronation Charter dealt (unavailingly) with the issues of relief, widows, and wardships of children later tackled in Magna Carta. This was why the 1100 charter was brought out again by the opposition to King John.

John's Angevin predecessors were also to blame. His father, Henry II (reigned 1154–89), had extended the royal forest, antagonizing wide sections of society. John's brother Richard I, between 1194 and 1199, had placed novel financial burdens on the country. The need for money to preserve the continental empire against the power of the king of France was a constant problem facing these kings. Another was that the great base of land brought to the monarchy by the Norman Conquest had slowly been eroded as land was given away to reward followers. As a result, kings had to exploit other, more politically sensitive, sources of revenue. Of course, the Angevins gave as well as took; they had developed immensely popular legal procedures that lay at the heart of what was later called 'the common law'. These were the assizes, which the charter sought to extend, not restrict. But here too was a problem, for the new procedures turned on due process of law. No free man was to lose his possessions 'unjustly and without judgement'. The year 1215 was the moment when society turned on the king and demanded that he obey his own rules.

Early in his reign John suffered two blows, first a rapid inflation for which he was blameless, and then, in 1204, the loss of Normandy. Thereafter he spent 'ten furious years' trying to raise the treasure to regain Normandy. The treasure went in an abortive military campaign in France of 1214. The grievances remained and produced Magna Carta.

OTHER KEY DATES IN THIS PERIOD

1204 **John loses Normandy.** Normandy was finally conquered by Philip II of France. This was a pivotal event in European history – now the cross-channel Anglo-Norman state was over. King and barons, like everyone else, would be born and live only in England. They had far more time for the affairs of Britain. The English conquest of Wales in the 1280s and near-conquest of Scotland around 1300 was the result.

1216 **Llywelyn dominates Wales.** Llywelyn ap Iorwerth, the ruler of Gwynedd, established his dominance over native Wales. His vision was of a principality in which he alone did homage to the king of England while the other native rulers did homage to him, in effect as prince of Wales. Two years later, in the Treaty of Worcester, Llywelyn's territorial conquests and practical (if not theoretical) supremacy were recognized by the king of England.

1217 **The throne is secured for John's son.** Two victories, the first at Lincoln, the second at sea off Sandwich, secured the throne for John's son, Henry III. Prince Louis, eldest son of Philip II of France, resigned his claims and returned to France. Had a French king ruled England, the political structure of Europe would have developed on incalculably different lines.

1221 **The friars move in.** The first Dominicans arrived in England, soon followed by the Franciscans. By around 1300 there were more than a hundred Dominican and Franciscan houses in Britain. With an emphasis on poverty, preaching and university study, they transformed the religious life of the island. A sermon by an educated preacher now became an everyday part of town life.

1225 **Magna Carta is reissued.** In 1216 and 1217 the minority government of Henry III had reversed John's policies and issued new versions of Magna Carta. In 1225, yet another version was issued in return for a heavy tax that saved the dynasty's continental possessions in Gascony. The

1225 version of the charter became definitive, the one confirmed by subsequent kings, clauses of which are on the statute book today.

1236 **A strong queen emerges.** Henry III married Eleanor of Provence, laying the foundations for a remarkable resurgence of queenly power. No queen consort had played a role in English political life since Eleanor of Aquitaine in the 1160s. Eleanor of Provence, made of far sterner stuff than her indulgent husband, changed that. Supporting, and supported by, her relations from Savoy, whom Henry established in England, she was a central figure in the politics of the reign.

1237 **Treaty of York.** Alexander II of Scotland resigned claims to the northern counties of England, which Scottish kings had pursued for 200 years. In return he gained substantial territory in Tynedale. He consolidated the Anglo-Scottish peace (it lasted from 1217 to 1296), and was free to concentrate on the conquest of Galloway, where he had taken armies in 1235 and 1236, thus extending the reach of the Scottish state.

1240 **End of a great Welsh leader.** This year marked the death of Llywelyn ap Iorwerth, justly called in his own lifetime Llywelyn the Great. His death ushered in a period in which the king of England recovered his power in Wales. But Llywelyn's vision of a Welsh principality under a single native ruler, the prince of Wales, was to be realized, if only for the ten years between 1267 and 1277, by his grandson.

1249 **Scotland loses King Alexander.** King Alexander II of Scotland (who had come to the throne aged 16 in 1214) died on an expedition to wrest lordship of the Isle of Man and the Hebrides from the king of Norway. The expedition summed up the way Alexander had re-oriented Scottish kingship. It would expand not south into England but north and west. The acquisition of Man and Hebrides was ultimately achieved by his son, Alexander III, securing Scotland's western borders. Together they had constructed a state strong enough to resist English attempts at conquest.

1295

Edward I goes on the warpath

MICHAEL PRESTWICH

England was prosperous in the thirteenth century, with a growing population. Great monastic estates, such as those of Winchester Cathedral Priory, or of the Cistercian monasteries of Yorkshire, were doing very well, as were the estates of earls and major barons. Some knightly families, however, found it increasingly hard to maintain their status in society. More and more land was put under the plough, as agricultural activity expanded to feed an increasingly numerous populace. Fenland was drained and exploited.

The wool trade was booming. Italian merchants were attracted to England; they provided credit mechanisms that helped to fuel the expansion of trade. The urban economy thrived. New towns continued to be founded – if not at quite the rate of the first half of the century – and established towns expanded. This was an economic expansion driven by a commercially minded populace, above all in England, but also in Scotland and Wales.

By 1295, however, there were beginning to be indications that population growth was no longer matched by the expansion of resources and by levels of investment. The years of prosperity were coming to an end.

The major political crisis of this half-century in England began in 1258, and lasted until 1265, when the baronial leader, Simon de Montfort, was killed at Evesham. Edward I did much to restore the prestige of the crown after he came to the throne in 1272, but in his later years he faced political difficulties. War meant heavy taxation, both on wool exports and on personal wealth.

Growing prosperity helped enable Edward I to extend his political influence in Britain. He conquered Wales in two campaigns, in 1277 and 1282–3; rebellion in 1294–5 saw the embers of resistance flare up. Scotland was a different story. Relations between England and Scotland were peaceable for most of the thirteenth century. Edward I oversaw the hearings of the Great Cause in 1291–2, which determined that John Balliol, not Robert Bruce, should be king after the death of the heiress Margaret, the Maid of Norway. Scotland's alliance with France led to Edward I's invasion in 1296, and Balliol's deposition, but in the next year William Wallace led a successful rebellion. The Wars of Independence had begun.

Relations with France were also peaceable until the 1290s. The war that began in 1294 was not of Edward I's choosing. He was tricked by French diplomacy into thinking that a marriage alliance was about to be agreed; instead the French moved into his duchy of Gascony. The war, which saw heavy expenditure but no major battles, lasted until a truce was agreed in 1297. It was a precursor of the Hundred Years War that began in 1337, though in that conflict the English claim to the French throne provided an additional element.

* * *

As the year 1295 opened, England's King Edward I and his troops were wintering in Conwy Castle, besieged by Welsh rebels. Food was running low; all the drink that remained was one small barrel of wine, left for the king's personal use. Edward had this distributed among his men, the action of a good commander.

The Welsh had been in rebellion since the previous autumn; they had taken advantage of English preoccupation with the war that had just started with France. The rising was a national one, headed by a then obscure figure, Madog ap Llywelyn. Wales had seemed conquered by 1283; now, the whole English achievement was under threat. Edward led a rapid raid from Conwy to the west, into the Lleyn peninsula, but it was elsewhere that the war was won. In March Madog was defeated in mid-Wales by forces under the earl of Warwick, at Maes Moydog. There, an English commentator noted that Madog's forces were 'the best and bravest Welsh that anyone has seen'. They met the English head on, but to no avail. English archers and men-at-arms were too powerful. Madog himself escaped. Edward went on a triumphant tour of Wales, receiving submissions from a defeated people. Eventually Madog was captured, and led to miserable captivity in the Tower of London.

The end of the Welsh rebellion was marked by the start of the building of a great new castle, Beaumaris in Anglesey, the last of the magnificent series of castles that marked Edward's conquest. It was characterized by concentric lines of defences, two great twin-towered gatehouses, and a dock so that ships could supply the fortress. Edward's great mason from Savoy, Master James of St George, was in charge of the project. In July the king returned from his circuit of Wales to see the work under way; accounts show that one evening there he enjoyed entertainment provided by an English harpist, Adam of Clitheroe.

Wales was only one of the immense problems that Edward faced; England's war with France was another. In the previous year the French had taken over much of Edward's duchy of Gascony in south-western France, and English forces there were hanging on with difficulty. His soldiers achieved a measure of success at the start of the year, but at Easter the French under Charles of Valois invaded. Rioms was besieged, and a sortie by the English garrison was driven back 'like sheep into the fold'. English holdings in Gascony were reduced to a couple of towns near Bordeaux, and Bayonne in the south.

To make things worse, the French took the war directly to the English. There was alarm in April when messengers reported that a large fleet was gathering across the Channel to attack England. In the event, attacks were more limited, but in August French galleys raided Dover, and the town of Winchelsea was assaulted. Royal proclamations declared that the English language itself was under threat from the French.

A spy scare heightened the atmosphere. A royal knight, Thomas Turberville, arrived in England claiming to have escaped from a French prison; in fact, he had been released on condition that he spied for the French. The report he wrote for them on the defenceless condition of the Isle of Wight, on English diplomacy and on preparations to send troops to Gascony was revealed to the king, and Turberville was arrested. After a trial he was drawn to the place of execution on an oxhide and hanged by an iron chain.

Edward's strategy was to build up a grand alliance in the Low Countries and Germany against the French. The duke of Brabant, Edward's son-in-law, came to Wales, and in Anglesey reached agreement to serve with 2,000 cavalry. The support of the counts of Guelders and Holland was bought, though in the latter case the count soon turned to the French. Most important was the count of Flanders, who was promised a huge subsidy. The French King Philip IV, however, summoned the count to Paris, and took his daughter hostage, so nullifying any English alliance. There was little hope of launching any expedition against Philip without Flemish support. Nonetheless, Edward had to continue to pay his remaining allies substantial sums.

Meanwhile, in Scotland, power was taken from the king, John Balliol, by his barons, and entrusted to a council. Balliol owed his throne to Edward I, who had supervised the hearings of the succession dispute between Balliol and Robert Bruce. Balliol was distrusted as an English puppet, and the Scots now looked to France for support. The French were anxious to acquire the Scots as allies against the English, and 1295 saw the alliance forged that would lead to war in the following year. In December Edward I issued writs summoning men to muster at Newcastle, ready for yet another war.

What Edward needed to fight his wars was money. Putting down the Welsh rebellion was an unexpected expenditure. The forces in Gascony were expensive to maintain, and the allies were hungry for English silver. The level of financial crisis is suggested by the sudden dismissal of the treasurer, William March, in August. Taxes had been granted in the previous year, but Edward needed a new instalment and Parliament was therefore summoned. It consisted of prelates and magnates, summoned from an established list, and representatives of shires and boroughs, as well as representatives of the clergy. A new formula was developed for the representatives; they were to come with full powers to represent their communities, and to do what was decided by common counsel.

This would remain the standard form of summons for many years, and led historians later to dub this parliament, held at Westminster in November and early December, the Model Parliament. It was not, of course, thought of as such at the time, and did not attract much attention from chroniclers. The tax that was granted would be levied on a valuation of people's personal property; the standard rate was an eleventh, but the towns and land that either was, or had been in the past, in the king's possession paid at a rate of a seventh.

While taxation was a major burden, recruitment was another. When Edward requested a group of nineteen magnates to go to Gascony, several, including the earl of Arundel, refused. Angrily, the king ordered the exchequer to collect any debts that they might owe to the crown. The men duly sailed. That was in August. In October orders went for the recruitment of a huge force of 25,000 infantry. The appointed commander of the English infantry was Edmund, earl of Lancaster, the king's brother. He, however, was in bad health, and departure was long delayed, into the next year.

In Norfolk Hugh Cressingham and William Mortimer arrived to collect troops for Gascony. Men were selected, and their local communities forced to pay for white tunics, swords and knives. Villages in one region produced roughly six men each. Some were sent home from the muster at Newmarket at once, as they were judged inadequate; others stayed four days, until the planned expedition was cancelled. A further burden was the compulsory purchase of foodstuffs by the crown, in support of its military efforts. Payment of money was disliked, but loss of carefully stored grain and other commodities was bitterly resented.

King Edward's relationship with the Church was difficult. A peace mission by two cardinals achieved nothing. In September a great ceremony took place at Canterbury, with the enthronement of a new archbishop, Robert Winchelsey, in the presence of the king and many nobles. It must have been an awkward occasion, for Edward was insistent that Winchelsey pay a substantial debt to the crown. In parliament, it proved hard to persuade the clergy to grant a tax of a tenth of their income.

This was not an easy year for the economy. Grain prices stood at high levels; poor weather meant a bad harvest. The thirteenth century had been one of expansion, as more and more land was put under the plough, but the boom years lay in the past. The main English export was wool, grown on the backs of some ten million sheep. Heavy customs duties, introduced in the previous year, combined with the war, had a serious effect on the level of exports. Italians had controlled much of the wool trade, but the great company of the Riccardi had been bankrupted in the previous year as a result of the war. They had lent heavily to Edward I, and their depositors in Italy were rightly suspicious, and withdrew their funds. The remaining companies in England were in an uncomfortable position, emphasized when in the autumn of 1295 they were threatened with the confiscation of the wool stocks they held.

This year showed how the English state could respond to the pressures of war. The need to obtain consent to taxation was important in the development of fully representative parliaments. The defeat of the Welsh rebellion marked a significant stage in the political unification of Britain, but events in Scotland pointed in a different direction, toward the Wars of Independence.

OTHER KEY DATES IN THIS PERIOD

1258 **The Provisions of Oxford**. There was much discontent, above all directed against Henry III's foreign favourites and his ambitious plan to obtain the Sicilian throne for his second son Edmund. A reform scheme was set up, which established a council of fifteen to control the king's actions. This was elected by twelve from the baronial side, and twelve from the royalists. Further important reform measures followed in the next year, with the Provisions of Westminster.

1265 **Battle of Evesham**. Simon de Montfort, leader of the baronial opposition, had triumphed in the previous year at Lewes. Now, he was defeated and slain at the hands of an army led by Henry III's son Edward. This marked the end of the reform movement, though there was some continued resistance, notably from the garrison of Kenilworth. Not all the ideas about reform, particularly of the law, were forgotten; some were to be followed up in Edward I's legislative programme.

1270 **Edward's crusade**. Edward joined crusading forces in North Africa. From there he went to Sicily, and then on to the Holy Land. Little was achieved in this expedition. Edward escaped assassination; the wound from his attacker's knife was sucked by his queen Eleanor (or, according to one account, by his friend Otto de Grandson). Edward did not return to England until 1274.

1275 **Institution of customs duties**. It was agreed in Parliament that six shillings and eight pence should be paid on each sack of wool exported from England. This provided the crown with a new, permanent financial resource. It was intended in the first instance to provide a means of repaying Italian merchants for the loans they had advanced to make the crusade possible, and was important in providing Edward I with the resources he needed for his wars.

1277 **First Welsh war**. Llywelyn ap Gruffudd, prince of Wales, had consistently refused to come to do homage to Edward I. Edward resorted to force to bring him to heel. The campaign saw the English march along the coast of North Wales, and invade Anglesey. There were no major battles, but Edward's show of strength was sufficient to make Llywelyn come to terms. Work began on four great new English castles, at Flint, Rhuddlan, Aberystwyth and Builth.

1282 Death of Llywelyn ap Gruffudd. The Welsh rebelled in this year, and Edward embarked on full-scale conquest. He advanced along the coast of North Wales, but Llywelyn broke out of Snowdonia and marched south. At Irfon Bridge he was defeated by an army led by lords of the Welsh March, and was slain in the battle, probably by Stephen Frankton, a squire. Llywelyn was succeeded by his brother Dafydd, who was thus the last native prince of Wales. He was captured in the following year, and was savagely executed at Shrewsbury.

1292 Hearing of the Great Cause. The Great Cause, the succession dispute in Scotland, concluded. The main rival claimants, on the death of Alexander III's heiress Margaret in 1290, were John Balliol and Robert Bruce. Edward I was invited to supervise the resolution of the dispute, and it was determined that the throne should go to Balliol. The decision may have been correct in law; it was also the one that suited Edward best.

1296 Invasion of Scotland. The French looked to the Scots as allies in their war against the English. The Anglo-Scottish war began with a small cross-border raid by the Scots; Edward I launched a major invasion. Berwick was sacked, with appalling scenes of slaughter. The English were then victorious at Dunbar, took Edinburgh, marched north as far as Elgin and deposed John Balliol. Success, however, was little more than superficial.

1297 Political crisis. Edward I faced the opposition of the Church and baronage to his campaign plans, and to the taxes and wool seizures needed for the financing of the expedition. The expedition went ahead, but the king had to concede that he would not impose such burdens again without the consent of the community of the realm.

1348

The Black Death hits Britain

W. MARK ORMROD

The Black Death was one of the greatest human tragedies ever experienced in the British Isles. Since the 1920s, historians have compared it to the First World War, so great was its demographic and psychological impact; more recently it has been analysed in relation to the advent of AIDS.

In fact, the scale and effect of the fourteenth-century disaster is still much disputed. How many people died, and how were the survivors affected? Did the Black Death really change the course of British social history, or merely accelerate trends that would have occurred anyway? In particular, historians have recently begun to consider whether it is appropriate to make comparisons with modern First World disasters because medieval people were much more conditioned and resigned to the notion that things have a tendency to fall apart.

The 'calamity-sensitive' nature of the medieval economy (a telling phrase) inured people to the prospect of hunger and disease in a way that would be unthinkable in modern Britain – even though it is still, of course, a daily reality in the Third World. Of all the outcomes of the Black Death, then, the one that is most difficult to fathom is probably the relative lack of comment on the disaster: when Geoffrey Chaucer wrote his *Canterbury Tales* he made only a single allusion to a phenomenon that contemporary society must surely have held as its greatest fear.

The plague was first reported in continental Europe in 1347 and reached Britain in the summer of 1348; the historical convention is that it entered England via the port of Melcombe Regis in Dorset. The name Black Death came later: at the time, people simply called this new disease the 'pestilence'. Although many different theories have been put forward, it seems most likely that the Black Death was bubonic plague, which is transmitted by fleas borne by rats; the apparent virulence of the outbreak of 1347–50 is explicable not only in terms of the lack of immunity among the population of Europe but also by the fact that the bubonic form may have been accompanied by outbreaks of pneumonic plague, which is spread by direct contagion between humans and which offered very little chance of survival. The plague raged in England over the second half of 1348 and on into 1349, then extended to Wales, Scotland and Ireland, and subsided during 1350.

Thanks to relatively good documentation, we can track the path of the plague quite closely in some parts of the country. Bishops' registers, which record the death and replacement of members of the clergy, and manor court rolls, which detail the transfer of tenancies on the deaths of holders, provide particularly detailed and time-specific evidence that has been the stock in trade of all modern historians of the plague. This and other statistical evidence is, inevitably, patchy. We know much more of what went on in England than in other parts of the British Isles.

In any case, one thing that is so difficult about the evidence is its typicality: it is well understood that, even within very particular localities, the impact of plague could vary considerably, ravaging some villages but leaving others untouched. A more general qualification is that in upland areas, which had a much smaller population scattered over isolated farmsteads, plague tended to have a proportionately smaller effect than in the nucleated villages and urban communities that were a feature of lowland Britain. All that said, it is now generally agreed, on the basis of the available statistical models, that the plague of 1348–50 carried off at least a third of the population of the British Isles.

If we ask how many people that proportion actually represents, we immediately get into much more difficult territory. There is no way of calculating precisely how many people lived in Britain in the fourteenth century. England – and more precisely lowland England – was clearly and by far the most populated part of the British Isles: indeed, it appears that some areas, especially in East Anglia and the area around the Wash, were supporting populations comparable with those of the same rural communities in the nineteenth century.

Historical orthodoxy currently has it that the population of England rose from about two million at the time of Domesday Book (1086) to perhaps six million in 1300, tailing off from that point and then plummeting dramatically in 1348–50. When we get to the English poll tax returns of 1377, we can extrapolate a population figure of about 2.75 million. By that point, Britain had experienced at least four visitations of plague – after the initial epidemic, there were other national outbreaks in 1360–1, 1368–9 and 1375. One of the important points about the Black Death, indeed, is the fact that it became endemic in Britain: outbreaks of plague – albeit often more localized – were a regular feature of life down to the Great Plague of London in 1665.

Those who experienced the great mortality of 1348–50

were already more than usually conscious of the fragility of their condition. The steady growth in the population over the previous centuries had put tremendous pressure on natural resources. Land already under the plough was farmed more intensively, and marginal land previously used only as pasture was increasingly turned over to the growing of cereals and pulses. In some parts of Britain, there was no further viable land available for arable farming. To maximize their profits from a hungry market, landlords gave up the traditional practice of allowing fields to lie fallow once every few years. In the absence of anything but the most basic of fertilizing techniques, however, the impact was simply to drain the soil of its goodness and, in the longer term, to reduce yields.

To all of these problems was added that most British of concerns, the weather. Around 1300, Europe entered a mini ice age that lasted until the seventeenth century. Longer, harsher winters and shorter, wetter summers impacted seriously on the agricultural economy. Between 1315 and 1322 harvests repeatedly failed, sending grain prices rocketing and leaving the poor with no means to feed themselves. Ten or even fifteen per cent of the population of England may have died from the effects of malnutrition during this period.

These natural disasters were compounded by human-made ones. Edward I's military interventions in Wales, Scotland and Ireland created a legacy of warfare that was deeply damaging to the economy. Farmers and merchants, the main taxpaying groups, groaned under the weight of new subsidies, while the Anglo-Scottish border suffered huge disruption as a result of the scorched-earth policies of armies on both sides. It is not surprising that the arrival of the Black Death in 1348 was seen as God's punishment on a people gone astray. For many, it seemed, quite literally, the end of the world.

This sense of looming disaster is captured most obviously and strikingly in the chronicles of the period. They show the sense of shock that ran through the elite as the plague made its inexorable path across the country. The death of the recently appointed archbishop of Canterbury, John Offord, was a particularly disarming event, demonstrating that not even the highest members of God's taskforce, the clergy, were immune from risk.

The genuine fright of the agricultural labour force was another preoccupation of monkish chroniclers, who resented the idea that their fields could not be ploughed and sown as normal. There are also hints at the moral issues raised by the plague. A few people followed the continental trend of seeking refuge in ostentatious penance through acts of public flagellation. Much more common in the years immediately after 1350 was the founding and joining of religious guilds as mutual societies designed to support their members' physical needs in this world and spiritual welfare in the next. Disapproving moralists noted, above all, the way that the peasantry, taking advantage of the low rents and high wages that resulted from a dramatic fall in the population, grew rich, lazy and uppity.

The last word – literally – is reserved for John Clynn, a Franciscan friar from Kilkenny. His chronicle represents the only detailed contemporaneous account of the effects of the Black Death in Ireland. Having recounted what he regarded as the especially severe ravages of the plague in the urban centres of Dublin and Drogheda, Clynn concluded his chronicle with a reflection on his own position, 'waiting among the dead for death to come', and offered the idea that he had provided additional unused parchment so that his work might be continued, 'if anyone is still alive in the future and any son of Adam can escape this pestilence'. Clynn's self-conscious preparation for the onset of the plague, to which he did indeed apparently succumb, is one of the most vivid memorials of the real terror and tragedy that was the Black Death.

* * *

The plague had a significant impact on the political map of England. The first half of the fourteenth century witnessed huge changes in the political makeup of the British Isles. At the beginning of the period, England's King Edward I (died 1307) appeared to be close to realizing his vision of a 'British empire'. He had subdued and assimilated the remaining independent enclaves in Wales, building the great ring of fortresses that survive as testimony to his favoured technique of rule by force.

He had also embarked on a war of conquest in Scotland and had begun to make significant gains there: in 1305 he put to death the Scottish insurgent William Wallace and instituted a new programme for the government of Scotland as an annexe of the English crown. The English lordship of Ireland, established since the twelfth century, apparently held firm. And Edward's successful defence of his dynastic possessions in the duchy of Aquitaine demonstrated the continued wider reach of Plantagenet rule.

By the end of the period, the picture was very different. Edward's son (Edward II, king 1307–27) and grandson (Edward III, king 1327–77) maintained a public commitment to English rule in Wales and Ireland. However, after the coronation of Robert the Bruce as an independent king of Scotland in 1306 and the English defeat at Bannockburn in 1314, the idea of direct English rule north of the Tweed became increasingly fantastical. In 1328 Edward III's government acknowledged Robert's son, David II, as an independent king, and although Edward extricated himself from this position in the 1330s, his declared aim was not to take over Scotland directly. Rather, he wanted to secure the succession of a new king, Edward Balliol, and revive the feudal lordship over the northern kingdom that had, in fact, been Edward I's original strategy.

The opening of Edward III's war with France in 1337, however, fundamentally changed the nature of the Plantagenet regime by drawing attention away from Edward I's notion of a united British Isles and focusing English ambitions on the revival of the Norman and Plantagenet empires in western and northern France.

The long-term impact can be seen in both practical and cultural ways. Except in the case of the Welsh longbowmen who played such an important part in the French wars, it was largely impossible by Edward III's reign for the English to move men, money and provisions between the further-flung corners of their British and continental territories.

More significantly still, the elites that ran England's dependencies no longer felt it necessary to identify with the fashion trends of the Westminster court. Within a generation the 'English of Ireland' would be condemned for sporting the dress and music of their adopted land. In Scotland and Wales the revival of 'native' customs by the aristocracy and gentry contributed significantly both to the preservation of ancient cultures and to the maintenance of a tradition of independence. Across the British Isles, the imperial strategies of Edward I can themselves be seen to have forged 'national' identities that were to challenge the political hegemony of English for centuries to come.

OTHER KEY DATES IN THIS PERIOD

1306 **Robert 'the Bruce' becomes king of Scots.** He launched a major challenge to Edward I of England's efforts to assimilate the northern kingdom into his 'British empire'. Having previously made significant inroads into Scotland and defeated and executed the rebel leader William Wallace in 1305, Edward's apparent invincibility now began to be questioned openly.

1307 **Death of Edward I** and accession of Edward II. Edward died at Burgh by Sands in Cumberland on his way to yet another campaign against the Scots. Although his reputation had become somewhat tarnished in his last years, at his death Edward was mythologized as a new Arthur and held up as a model of kingship for his successors. Edward II made an unpromising start to his reign and was soon locked in political dispute with the barons over the influence of his favourite, Piers Gaveston, whom they put to death in 1312.

1314 **Battle of Bannockburn.** Edward II's forces suffered a humiliating defeat by Robert the Bruce. The Scots made effective use of the *shiltrom*, a tightly packed contingent of infantry pikemen; English cavalry forces proved ill-disciplined and many prominent knights were cut down. Edward II's subsequent withdrawal from Scotland left significant parts of northern England vulnerable to regular and devastating Scottish raids and created much political discontent.

1320 **Declaration of Arbroath.** A group of Scotland's political leaders appealed to the pope for assistance, declaiming – in words that have had resonance ever since – that 'as long as a hundred of us are left, we will never submit on any condition to English rule'.

1327 **Deposition of Edward II,** accession of Edward III. The disastrous and tyrannical regime of Edward II and his cronies, the Despensers, was brought to a violent close in a coup led by his own wife, Isabella, and her lover, Roger Mortimer. Edward, taken prisoner while fleeing through Wales, was forced to abdicate the throne and was imprisoned at Berkeley Castle. A parliament called in the name of his 14-year-old son was summoned to Westminster and the new regime of Edward III began. Edward II was subsequently murdered and buried at Gloucester Abbey (now the cathedral), though some historians suggest that he escaped to the Continent. Isabella and Mortimer ran the country for three years, but in 1330 Edward III launched an attack on Mortimer at Nottingham Castle, put him to trial and execution, and assumed control of his regime.

1328 **Treaty of Edinburgh**. The new regime of Edward III acknowledged the independence of Scotland. The following year, Robert the Bruce died, succeeded by his young son David II. Later, in 1333, Edward III reopened the war in support of a rival claimant for the throne, Edward Balliol.

1337 **Beginning of the Hundred Years War**. Tensions between the English and French crowns over the Plantagenet possessions in Aquitaine had rumbled on since the Treaty of Paris of 1259, and the English argued that the duchy should be theirs in full sovereignty, not a fief held under the lordship of the king of France. In 1337 Edward III renounced his homage to Philip VI of France for the duchy and set about defending his rights there by force; for the first years of the war, however, diplomatic and military strategy was focused on the Low Countries and northern France. In 1340 Edward announced himself king of France by right of descent, through his mother, from the house of Capet.

1346 **Battles of Crécy and Neville's Cross**. Edward III achieved a major victory over France's Philip VI at Crécy. His commanders in northern England captured David II of Scotland at Neville's Cross. These victories transformed Edward's status, and the reputation of his armies, throughout Europe.

1348 **Foundation of the Order of the Garter**. Edward III celebrated his recent military successes by setting up what remains today as England's oldest and most important order of chivalry.

1381

Peasants rise in revolt

CAROLINE BARRON

Throughout the British Isles in the later fourteenth century the standard of living was rising as the population decline brought about by the Black Death of 1347–50 led to an increase in per capita wealth. But in England, in particular, this increased prosperity was eroded by the rising costs of the war with France. Edward III's early aggressive campaigns onto French soil, which had yielded prestige, booty and ransoms, were now replaced by a more defensive, and expensive, strategy. The French had turned the tables and in the 1370s raided the south coast of England, burning Rye and Winchelsea. In the last decade of his reign, Edward III withdrew from government, his son the Black Prince died in 1376 and his young grandson, Richard II, at the age of 11 succeeded him as king of England in 1377. He inherited a rich country saddled with an unwinnable war.

The personal prosperity produced by the population decline led to increased self-confidence and social unrest. Since the thirteenth century there had been localized protests against the demands by manorial lords for compulsory services (serfdom), but protests had become more frequent since the Black Death had shifted the balance of power away from manorial lords in favour of labourers and craftsmen. These protests were becoming more sophisticated as peasants hired lawyers to argue that their particular manor had once formed part of the royal estate (where all men were free). As a result, the Commons claimed in the Parliament of 1377 that villeins (serfs) had 'withdrawn the customs and services due to their lords, holding that they are completely discharged of all manner of service due both from their persons and their holdings'.

All over Europe, in Paris in 1358, in Florence and Ghent in 1378, groups of protesters were making their voices heard in armed clamour. There is no single explanation for this volley of protests, since the pressures of population decline, price fluctuations, the imposition of taxation, the spread of literacy and the consequences of warfare affected different groups in different ways. But what was unique about the 1381 rising in England was that it was the only one that was truly national: it was the most widespread and the most coordinated. Crucially, the small size of England and its centralized government provided the protesters with a single objective: the king and his council.

* * *

In June 1381 thousands of men – and some women – from south-east England converged on London in a mass armed protest. The young king, Richard II, was virtually held hostage in the Tower, some of his leading councillors were murdered in the streets of London, and the news of the rising sparked off other localized protests further afield. This mass protest, popularly known as the Peasants' Revolt, has achieved iconic status in the English political memory, more recently in the protests organized to resist the proposed new community charge (aka the poll tax) in

1990. The revolt was extremely important but not necessarily for the reasons for which it is remembered.

It was called the Peasants' Revolt because that is how the hostile monastic chroniclers viewed it: a revolt of the *rustici* who were, in their eyes, scarcely human. But any revolt on a mass scale in late medieval England was bound to be composed of country people since they comprised over 90 per cent of the population. Thus there could be no mass revolt in which they did not participate. Moreover it is clear that many who were not 'peasants' also took part: local gentry and knights, townspeople and clergy. These were not the poor and downtrodden but men whose social status did not correspond to their prosperity. People from all social groups, except perhaps the aristocracy, were involved.

It is hard to discern the objectives of the protesters, but there are routes into an understanding of their motives. Two sets of 'Demands', apparently presented to the king in mid-June, have been preserved in chronicle accounts. On the first occasion the protesters asked for freedom from serfdom and a standard rent for land of 4d an acre; on the second, the demand for the abolition of serfdom was repeated, along with the demand for an end to lordship and the redistribution of ecclesiastical property among the people of the parish. On neither occasion was there any reference to the poll tax or to the burdens of taxation.

The organizers of the rising chose to focus on the day of the Christian festival of Corpus Christi, which was always marked throughout England by communal activity such as processions. In 1381 the feast fell on Thursday 13 June. The trigger for the risings seems to have been the activities late in May of justices of the peace at Brentwood in Essex who were enquiring into poll tax evasion. The third poll tax (or per capita tax) had been agreed by Parliament in November 1380. All lay people (the clergy were separately taxed) over the age of 15 were to pay three groats each (one shilling), which amounted to about one week's wages. Only genuine paupers were to be excused. But, as was usual with medieval taxation, it was expected that the rich would help the poor, and in many places this happened. This was the heaviest of the three poll taxes, however, and there was considerable evasion, hence the commissions of inquiry. When Sir Robert Bealknap, the king's chief justice, rode into Essex to help the local justices he was nearly ambushed, and 'travelled home as quickly as possible'. The rising had begun.

The first rebels arrived at Blackheath from Kent on Wednesday 12 June. John Ball, whose unorthodox preaching had earlier landed him in Maidstone Prison, was now released by the rebels and at Blackheath preached on the theme: 'When Adam delved and Eve span, Who was then the gentleman?' The aim of the rebels was to meet the king and explain to him their grievances, and to remove those councillors around him whom they held responsible for the failures in the French war, the heavy taxation and the judicial injustices that they suffered. Richard, standing in a barge in mid-stream at Greenwich, received the list of the nine 'traitors' whose heads the rebels wanted. These included Richard's uncle John of Gaunt (luckily for him he was away from London negotiating a truce with the Scots), the chancellor (Simon Sudbury, archbishop of Canterbury), the treasurer (Robert Hales), the chief justices, as well as local officials in Kent and Essex. When Richard refused their demands the rebels swarmed towards London. They opened prisons, sacked the archbishop's palace at Lambeth, destroying manorial documents, and burned the Savoy Palace of John of Gaunt. From the security of the Tower, Richard and his councillors looked out on the smoking buildings and the fires of the rebels camped on Tower Hill.

The following day Richard, leaving behind the unpopular councillors, rode out with a small entourage to try to draw the rebels off to Mile End. It was recognized that the rebels had no hostility to Richard himself, and when he arrived at Mile End the king was treated respectfully. When the rebels asked for the abolition of serfdom Richard agreed that charters of manumission (i.e. granting personal freedom) should be written out. And this was indeed done. Satisfied, the Mile End rebels began to disperse. Richard's decoy action had not saved two of his men, though: the rebels who had not gone to Mile End broke into the Tower and dragged Archbishop Sudbury and Treasurer Hales out to be executed on Tower Hill.

Saturday 15 June marked the climax of the rising in London. Richard rode out once more to meet the rebels, this time at Smithfield. Here the rebels were led by Wat Tyler, who treated the king in a familiar way and called him 'brother'. Although Richard granted the new demands of the rebels, 'saving his regality', a scuffle broke out. Tyler was mortally wounded and as he rode back towards his companions, he fell from his horse. At this moment of tension, Richard rode out and called to the rebels, 'I will be your king, your captain and your leader. Follow me.' And he led them away from the City to Clerkenwell Fields. The mayor of London later dragged Tyler into Smithfield, where he was executed. When Richard met his mother that night he told her he had 'recovered my inheritance, the realm of England, which I had nearly lost'. As indeed was true.

As soon as the king and his councillors had regained the upper hand, the retribution began. Although the rebellion in Kent died down quite rapidly, the embers continued to smoulder in Essex. On 28 June the remaining rebel army was easily defeated, and on 2 July the king revoked all the charters of freedom and pardon that he had granted. Commissions were appointed to collect accusations against the rebels and, in all, several hundred were executed.

Although the rising in the summer of 1381 had a cascade effect on other parts of England – there were protests as far away as Cornwall and Yorkshire – there were no repercussions in other parts of the British Isles. The Black Death had struck Scotland, Wales and Ireland as fiercely as in England, yet their social structures and economies were different. In Scotland, for example, personal servitude had disappeared by the mid-fourteenth century: Scottish lords exploited their rural workers in different ways, but there was a conscious decision to avoid heavy taxation. In all three countries protest took the form of a heightened national consciousness rather than class warfare. So the pressures that led to the rising in England, in the rest of the British Isles led to renewed struggles against the English, seen most forcefully in the revolt of Owain Glyn Dŵr in Wales.

On the face of it, the rising of 1381 appears to have achieved nothing. So why is it a turning point? It did not lead to a statute abolishing serfdom but it did lead lords to take the safer course and, instead of farming their demesne lands with unwilling servile labour, they leased the lands and lived on the rents rather than the produce. In this way villein tenure (land held in return for compulsory labour services) disappeared, although personal serfdom or bond status remained. As late as 1549 the rebels who followed Robert Kett demanded that 'all bondmen may be made free'. It largely ceased to matter, but the status survived as an instrument of extortion since men would pay large sums to be free of the stigma of servile status. It is true that no English government – until 1990 – again attempted to introduce per capita taxation. The attempt of the medieval poll taxes to spread taxation more widely failed because the burden was not also spread more equitably: the rich paid less, proportionately, than the poor. So this novel form of taxation was discredited.

The English rising of 1381 was a turning point because it destroyed the complacency of the English ruling classes and in so doing it ensured that those who ruled England must in future be responsive to the wider political community. Those who governed England and those who owned the land were conscious, even if they could not bring themselves to admit it, that the despised *rustici* were capable of bringing the realm to its knees and that they had the organizational and military skills, and literacy, to bring this about.

Just as 9/11 brought home to western governments not only the strongly held views of Islamic believers but also the ability of Islamic extremists to organize protests on a massive scale, so too in 1381 the followers of John Ball and Wat Tyler demonstrated that they could make their voices heard. In future English governments chose to listen.

OTHER KEY DATES IN THIS PERIOD

1356 **Battle of Poitiers.** Edward the Black Prince, when successfully raiding French territory from Gascony on 18 September, collided, near Poitiers, with the French army led by their king, John. The following day, more by luck than strategy, Edward, 'fighting like a cruel lion', defeated the French and took their king prisoner. This marked a high point in English ambitions in France but proved to be only a flash in the pan.

1359 **Birth of Owain Glyn Dŵr.** He claimed the title prince of Wales in September 1400 and led the most successful rebellion against English rule in Wales since the conquest of 1282. Owain summoned a Welsh Parliament, promoted the Welsh language and proposed to set up two universities in his principality. But after 1406 the revolt degenerated into guerrilla warfare that ended with Owain's death in around 1416.

1376 **The Good Parliament.** In this 'great' Parliament the Commons seized the initiative, led by their speaker, Peter de la Mare, and devised a new procedure 'in common' – impeachment – to challenge the corrupt and self-seeking councillors around the ageing King Edward III. For the first time in fifty years they refused to make a grant of taxation. Their self-assertion was to echo down the years.

1377 **The London 'Jubilee Book'.** The citizens of London drafted a new constitution for the city, known as the 'Jubilee Book' since it was put together in the fiftieth year of Edward III's reign. Job descriptions for city officers (in the form of oaths) and procedures for election were written down to make civic government more accessible. But this attempt at transparency led to acute factionalism and the Jubilee Book was publicly burnt in 1387.

1387 **The Canterbury Tales.** Although Geoffrey Chaucer began to write his best-known work in this year, it was still incomplete when he died in October 1400. Undoubtedly the greatest medieval English poet, Chaucer raised the status of English as a language fit for courtly literature, and made it a vehicle for poetry that could also be read privately for personal enjoyment.

1388 **Battle of Otterburn.** The Scots, led by James, earl of Douglas (who was killed in the battle) inflicted a notable defeat on the English at Chevy Chase, in which Henry Hotspur, son of the earl of Northumberland, was captured. The defeat ended the domination of the northern border by the Percy earls of Northumberland. The subsequent truce severed the Franco-Scottish alliance that had seriously damaged the English war effort.

1394 **English expedition to Ireland.** Richard II was the first English king to lead an expedition to Ireland since 1210, and the last to do so until William III fought the Battle of the Boyne nearly 300 years later. The Gaelic chiefs were persuaded to become royal vassals, royal authority extended beyond the Pale and, for a brief time, much of Ireland was incorporated into the British political system.

1395 **The 'Twelve Conclusions' of the Lollards.** The Lollards nailed their outspoken criticisms of the Church, written in Latin and in English, to the doors of Westminster Hall and St Paul's when Parliament was sitting. These 'Conclusions' reflected the populist interpretations of the ideas of John Wycliffe (died 1384) and provoked a sharp clerical backlash. The criticisms continued, though, and finally triumphed in the Reformation of the 1540s.

1399 **Deposition of Richard II.** Henry Bolingbroke deposed his cousin Richard as king of England by a blatant act of force, which his garbled claim citing rightful descent and divine favour barely concealed. The deposition of the legitimate king seriously damaged royal authority and ultimately exposed England to the miseries of the civil wars known as the Wars of the Roses.

1415

Henry V takes the field at Agincourt

RALPH GRIFFITHS

The battle of Agincourt on 25 October 1415 was the climax of Henry V's first invasion of France. The English victory was overwhelming, while Henry's role in the fighting secured his reputation as a military genius blessed by God. It was a turning point in the king's life and in his quest to be king of France as well as England. The year was also critical for his kingdom and its relationship with Wales, Scotland and Ireland, as well as for its European reputation, as preparations for the campaign brought to a head issues that influenced developments for a long time afterwards.

Soon after Henry became king in March 1413 at the age of 25, he began preparing for an invasion of France, which he had advocated in his father's reign. Preparations included securing the Welsh and Scottish borders and strengthening England's military and naval capabilities. The king combined the self-confidence and ambition of youth with single-minded purpose and military experience gained in Wales against Owain Glyn Dŵr. In 1414,

Henry's intentions became clearer and after Parliament met in November, MPs could report to their constituencies that he would soon be taxing his subjects and the Church and seeking loans to raise an army larger (at 12,000 combatants) than any since the 1346 Crécy campaign of his great-grandfather, Edward III, who had staked a claim to the French throne in 1340.

Henry's ultimate objective, and his obligation as Edward's heir, was the French crown. More immediately, and realistically, he tried to force territorial concessions from the elderly and insane French monarch, Charles VI, and his quarrelsome nobility: it was the best time to invade France. Henry and Charles exchanged ambassadors over many months, but the French could not agree to the ever-increasing English demands. Meanwhile, Henry was planning to shock the French with his power. By mid-March 1415, Charles realized that invasion was coming and negotiations could only delay it. In April and May Henry proclaimed that 'we, with God's help, are about to go overseas to recover and regain the inheritances and just rights of our crown, which, as everyone agrees, have long been unjustly withheld.'

At the same time, Henry's enterprise put great strains on England, its men, money and loyalties, especially because he might be absent for as long as a year. These strains showed themselves during 1414–15; the way in which they were managed helped to ensure astonishing successes for the English that continued even after the king's early death in 1422.

The army of 1415 was mostly recruited in central and southern England, and the king's lands in Lancashire, Cheshire and South Wales provided its mainstay, archers. Though the Welsh revolt petered out after 1409, Glyn Dŵr was at large until 1416 and there was resentment that had to be overcome if the king wanted to impose war taxation

in Wales and raise Welsh soldiers. Thus, soon after he
became king, Henry aimed to draw a line under the revolt.
He even made overtures to Glyn Dŵr in July 1415, a month
before embarkation. Service in France and loyalty to the
king benefited Welsh soldiers on their return and, in the
longer term, reconciled Welsh families to English rule.
The crown's second dominion, Ireland, was also a
problem. Glyn Dŵr tried to ally with independent Irish
chieftains who resented Anglo-Irish lords and English gov-
ernors in Dublin, and might assist England's French and
Scottish enemies. Moreover Ireland, more so than Wales,
was a drain on English resources; when Henry V gave priority in men and money to the French war, the lordship
of Ireland gradually fell under the control of Anglo-Irish
lords. This detached Ireland from effective English rule
during the rest of the century.
The separate kingdom of Scotland was a greater threat.
From the fourteenth century, the Auld Alliance between
France and Scotland gave every English king who planned
to campaign in France pause for thought that the Scots
might launch raids, or worse, across the border. Henry V
inherited one advantage from his father: King James I of
Scotland had been a prisoner in England since 1406. Yet
this did not deter the Scots, for the duke of Albany, the
regent of Scotland, was not keen to negotiate James' return,
even though his own son, Murdach, was also imprisoned
in England. In November 1414 Parliament took steps to
defend Berwick and the borders, and Henry tried to come
to terms with Albany by exchanging Murdach for Henry
Percy, heir to the earldom of Northumberland, who had
been in Scottish hands since 1402. This agreement would
have been a useful insurance in 1415, but the exchange was
postponed and shortly before Henry embarked for France,
French envoys arrived in Scotland (22 June); a month
later a Scottish force crossed the border and the English

retaliated. The French war increased tension between England and Scotland, and Scots even served in French armies after 1419.

Of course, Henry had to stamp his authority on England if he were to campaign in France – especially so early in his reign. His father Henry IV had seized the crown from Richard II in 1399 but this act, which founded the Lancastrian dynasty, did not go unchallenged and he spent much of his reign fighting rebellions. When Henry V succeeded in 1413, some claimed that the deposed Richard II was still alive, and others believed that Edmund Mortimer, earl of March, was his rightful heir. Henry also faced trouble from Lollard heretics inspired by John Wycliffe (died 1384), whose calls for Church reform were regarded as traitorous, especially when, in January 1414, the king's friend, Sir John Oldcastle, joined a rising. Parliament passed anti-Lollard legislation, and early in 1415 the execution of heretics in London gripped the public and the city chroniclers – and helped Henry harness the Church in support of his war.

Oldcastle escaped and by August 1415 was causing trouble in the Welsh borderland, just when a plot against the king was being hatched. These threats to Lancastrian rule were not coordinated but Henry V's war preparations gave them focus. The plot aimed to kill the king at Southampton and place the young earl of March on the throne; but it was nipped in the bud, and the Agincourt victory ended for a generation all serious challenges to Henry and his son Henry VI that had used the revolution of 1399 as justification. The leading plotters were the earl of Cambridge, Lord Scrope of Masham and Sir Thomas Grey of Northumberland, hoping that March would attract support in Wales and Scotland. At the last moment (31 July), March himself revealed all to the king and the leaders were summarily executed; Henry left it to Parliament in his absence to endorse what he had done. The treatment of the plotters and the presence of most nobles in the English army reflect Henry's success in mastering his enemies and reconciling dissidents. Victory at Agincourt induced Church and Parliament to support future campaigns.

Agincourt entered English (and Welsh) mythology because contemporaries celebrated it, exaggerated Henry's achievement and saw God's hand in it all, and because Shakespeare's vision has been compelling drama ever since. But it was close run. Henry's army left Southampton on 11 August, late in the season for a long campaign. It made for Harfleur on the river Seine, rather than English Calais, presumably 'to stuff the town with Englishmen' so Normandy could be overawed, the Channel secured and communications with Aquitaine established.

The army found the town of Harfleur heavily fortified, however, and the siege was long and disease-ridden; a third of the army either died or was invalided home with dysentery. The town eventually surrendered on 22 September after heavy bombardment. The decision to march through Normandy to Calais turned out to be dangerous. Henry's exhausted army, perhaps 9,000 men, mostly archers, had difficulty in finding a safe crossing of the river Somme, so that instead of covering 150 miles, they marched 250 miles in seventeen days, allowing a larger French army to overtake them. In the heat of battle at Agincourt, moreover, Henry flouted chivalric convention by slaughtering many captives. But his victory on 25 October swept all criticism aside.

To an English observer, the French seemed 'like a countless swarm of locusts', but they were not led by their king or his heir, and most of the royal dukes were absent. Henry donned his helmet with 'a very rich crown of gold encircling it like an imperial crown', and delivered a speech to his men: 'In the name of Almighty God, and of St George, Forward Banner! And St George this day thine help.' The

French cavalry was dislocated by English and Welsh archers and the hand-to-hand fighting was ferocious. The French dead were piled to the height of a man's head; the losses on the English side were astonishingly small. To the English, this seemed God's work.

Agincourt was not a decisive battle, although Harfleur's capture was important. For the French, the battle was devastating to morale. For the English, it became the stuff of patriotic propaganda focused on Henry V and binding nobles, churchmen and Parliament to his causes. He was reportedly carried ashore at Dover on the shoulders of exultant subjects; in London on 23 November pageants proclaimed, 'Blessed is he who comes in the name of the Lord.' Agincourt helped to create a regal myth that sustained the king and his French enterprise – and made subsequent defeats seem all the more scandalous.

On the Continent, the reputation of England and its king was transformed. At the Church Council at Constance (1414–18), English envoys lauded 'our victorious king of England, Henry V, faithful soldier of Christ and strongest striver after peace'. Sigismund, emperor of Germany, visited Henry in May 1416 to make peace between England and France, and went away his ally. In Italy the king was known as Il Magnifico. Agincourt's memory spurred Henry to renew hostilities in 1417, leading to the conquest of Normandy and the 1420 Treaty of Troyes, which recognized him as heir to the French throne. The year 1415 was when the Lancastrian dynasty was stabilized at home and set out on extraordinarily ambitious paths abroad.

OTHER KEY DATES IN THIS PERIOD

1400 **Henry subdues the Scots.** After seizing Richard II's crown, Henry IV faced serious difficulties. A conspiracy to assassinate him at Windsor was thwarted at the last moment, and the nobles involved were killed at Cirencester (January). Richard II's murder at Pontefract (February) outraged many; in the summer Henry led an army to subdue the Scots; and in September Owain Glyn Dŵr declared himself prince of Wales, prompting Henry to lead his first expedition against the Welsh.

1401 **Licence to burn.** The statute 'on the burning of heretics' enabled the first English Lollard, William Sawtre, to be burned at Smithfield (March). It authorized relapsed heretics to be punished by a government that feared insurrection as well as criticism of the Church.

1403 **Battle of Shrewsbury.** By quick and decisive action, Henry IV defeated Henry Hotspur and his father Northumberland, who had Welsh and Scottish support, at the battle of Shrewsbury (July). This marked the beginning of the king's long but successful campaign to quell rebellion against him.

1412 **The first Scottish university is founded.** Scotland's first university was founded at St Andrews and received authorization from Pope Benedict XIII. Before this, Scottish students went to continental (especially French) universities for their education and religious training during the wars with England.

1420 **Henry V becomes duke of Normandy.** The notable Treaty of Troyes between Henry V and Charles VI of France (May) was the pinnacle of Henry V's achievement. It recognized him as duke of Normandy and heir to the French throne, and in June he married Charles' daughter Catherine. The dauphin was disinherited and Henry and Charles entered Paris together on 12 December. Henry V died two months before

Charles VI (in 1422), so that the 'dual kingdom' was inherited instead by the nine-month-old Henry VI.

1429 **The right to vote is defined.** A statute of the English Parliament defined the qualification for voting in county elections: it was limited to freeholders with property worth forty shillings net per annum and was probably designed to raise the standing of MPs and to avoid disputed elections. The statute remained in force until the 1832 Reform Act.

1440 **Eton and King's College, Cambridge are founded.** Henry VI founded Eton College for twenty-five poor scholars, the first English king to found a public grammar school with educational and religious objectives. Four months later (February 1441) he also founded King's College, Cambridge. They were among a number of such foundations in mid-fifteenth-century England.

1483

Richard III snatches the crown

CHRISTINE CARPENTER

England in 1450 was a much-governed country. Kings could raise large sums for war by taxation, they took responsibility for law and peacekeeping and were becoming involved in economic and moral regulation. There was a sizeable and expert central bureaucracy but most government was done by local amateurs, usually gentry, the local nobility playing a large part in coordinating their activities. One effect of the extended period of crisis was to reduce the regional authority of the nobles, putting kings more directly in command of governance in the shires. This is no longer seen as the replacement of a corrupt system of government, loosely referred to as 'bastard feudalism', by something more 'modern' and it is now understood that direct and indirect rule both had their strengths and weaknesses.

The European-wide economic depression, caused by plague-induced demographic decline and a bullion shortage, was at its worst in 1450. In England prices and agrarian incomes were low. Towns, after a period of expansion, were mostly in decline, as was international trade. However, late in the century, the cloth trade, England's principal export, recovered. For the lower classes, though, times were good: real wages had risen significantly in town and country, serfdom had virtually disappeared, land was available cheaply and on good terms. Enterprising yeoman farmers, exploiting the more buoyant parts of the agrarian market, could prosper. Despite all this decline, London continued to grow as an economic, political and cultural centre.

Full literacy was the norm among the middling and upper classes, while there were enough readers among the lower classes for even the illiterate to have access to the written word. Certainly, the English populace was politically well informed. The religion of the English, however, was conventional, there were very few heretical Lollards, and, from top to bottom of society, gifts were made to religious institutions, most often to the parish church.

Defeat in 1453 ended the Hundred Years War, despite Edward IV's failed efforts to restart it in 1475. That made it easier to neglect Scotland, France's traditional ally, and political upheavals in England diverted attention from the British Isles in general.

By 1450 Wales was becoming Anglicized, with its own squirearchy, but the political crisis affected Wales as well as England and there was a descent into disorder, halted only under Edward IV. Much of Ireland was already out of English control but, from the 1470s, Edward and then Henry tried to restore some order, especially in making the remaining core of English settlement, the Pale, more secure. This was done by a combination of alliances with great Anglo-Irish nobles, like the Butlers and the Fitzgeralds, and periodic expeditions from England, the trend being towards greater external intervention. Perhaps partly because of the absence of English attacks, Scotland in this period was peaceful compared with England – just one king, James III, was violently removed and that was by his son – and kings usually won in confrontations with their nobles. Apart from offering half-hearted support for the Lancastrians in the early 1460s, Scottish kings in this period generally preferred diplomacy to war in dealing with England.

* * *

Not so long ago, everyone would have agreed that the turning point of this period was 1485, when Henry VII won the crown at the battle of Bosworth and the Tudor dynasty began. This used to be seen as the point when the modern history of England started, as the struggle between Yorkist and Lancastrian factions in the Wars of the Roses came to a close. More recently, however, historians have been noting the similarities between the rule of the Yorkists (the dynasty that controlled the country from the accession of Edward IV in 1461 to the death of Richard III in 1485) and of Henry VII (reigned 1485–1509). Moreover it has become clear that the economic, social, religious and cultural history of England from the mid-fifteenth to the early sixteenth centuries shows considerable continuity. There is thus a good case for the date that has increasingly become the starting point for the new periodization: 1461, when the Yorkists came to the throne.

However, there was initially no certainty about the survival of the new dynasty and, since the century ended with a Tudor rather than a Yorkist on the throne, to take 1461 as the key year would be paradoxical. The choice of 1483 answers the objections to both 1485 and 1461. By 1483, the Yorkist dynasty was firmly established and apparently secure and yet in that year the seeds of its destruction two years later were sown. What happened in 1485 was the almost inevitable result of Richard III's usurpation in 1483.

In 1461, Edward of York defeated the forces of the Lancastrian Henry VI and became Edward IV. He had the support of only a small number of the nobility and almost none of the major nobles, apart from the Nevilles, the greatest of whom was Richard, earl of Warwick, 'the Kingmaker'. Indeed, it was not until 1471 that Edward could truly count himself king. This was after he had been briefly replaced by Henry VI, in a French-backed rebellion instigated by Warwick, in which Edward's own brother, the duke of Clarence, participated. Henry VI, his son Edward of Lancaster, and Warwick all died in this rebellion, giving Edward a clean slate.

So effective was Edward's rule in what is known as his second reign that, by 1483, his ability to impose his will on the country was possibly greater than that of any king since Edward I (died 1307). At its heart were two interlinked forces: a close-knit nobility, among whom his ultra-loyal youngest brother, Richard of Gloucester, the greatest power in the north, was the most prominent; and a powerful household and affinity, led by Lord Hastings, Edward's oldest and truest political ally. The royal finances and internal order had been restored after the downward spiral of both under Henry VI, and Edward was far too secure for foreign powers to try to intervene in English affairs. Indeed, in his second reign, he was pardoning and restoring some of the exiled Lancastrians and, towards the end of the reign, Henry Tudor, long exiled in France, was considering relinquishing his claim as the heir of Lancaster and returning to England. The succession seemed secure with Edward's two healthy sons.

Then, on 9 April Edward died unexpectedly, shortly before his forty-first birthday. The age of his heir, Edward V, made it difficult to set up a stable minority government. At 12 he was too young to rule but too close to the age when he might begin to do so. Even so, all would be well as long as the three centres of power could work together. These were the Woodvilles, Edward V's mother's family, who controlled the king's person; Hastings, linchpin of the royal household and political connection; and Gloucester, with his great territorial power. The young king was at Ludlow and, as his Woodville relatives were bringing him to London for his coronation, they were met at Stony Stratford by Richard of Gloucester and his new ally, the duke of Buckingham. There, on 30 April, Edward was forcefully removed from his entourage, and some of the Woodvilles arrested and later executed. Nevertheless, Gloucester continued to work with Hastings, whose control of the royal household gave him enormous power around the king and in the localities, and to prepare for the coronation. But on 13 June Hastings was seized and executed. Gloucester, who had thus removed the opposition first of Edward V's family and then of the Yorkist political and military establishment, took the throne on 26 June. Richard III, as he now was, justified his usurpation by the need for continuity. However, he had done the hitherto unthinkable: he had deposed a king who had not just done no wrong but had not been in a position to do anything at all, and who had succeeded a successful king.

Richard's immediate problem was that he was heavily reliant on his closest accomplices, notably Buckingham, and could only keep their support by bribing them with grants. In October Buckingham, having decided Richard was not giving him enough, rebelled. But the core of the rebellion was the Yorkist household. This had originally acquiesced, probably partly taken by surprise and partly in the hope of saving the princes, but, by October, there had been time to resolve to resist Richard and it was probably known by then that the princes were dead.

Rebellion was therefore raised in the name of Henry Tudor and, almost overnight, the man who had given up hope of pursuing his claim to the throne became the Yorkist claimant; to enhance his appeal, he promised to marry Edward IV's daughter, Elizabeth, if he became king. The rebellion failed and a number of Yorkists left England, followed by others as Richard III's short reign progressed.

In late 1483, as his support outside the north dwindled, Richard had to embark on a policy of 'planting' northern supporters throughout the Midlands and the south, using lands and offices confiscated from Yorkists. These northern interlopers not only earned him a great deal of resentment but also stretched his resources of reliable manpower. In a vicious circle, as Richard's support diminished, so he became less viable as a king and more people deserted. By the time of Henry Tudor's invasion and the battle of Bosworth in 1485, this disbelief and disaffection had spread across much of England, even into Richard's northern stronghold.

Richard might possibly still have won at Bosworth, but Henry was only in a position to defeat him because of what had happened between 1483 and 1485. Moreover, the unease in Richard's forces, and late betrayal by some of his supposed allies, both of which contributed to his defeat, are also directly attributable to the diminution of belief in his kingship whose roots lay in the way he had taken the throne in 1483. If Bosworth was a Lancastrian victory, it was even more the restoration of the Yorkist establishment.

Why Richard acted can never be known but, since he had shown no previous signs of uncontrollable ambition, it is probable that he was impelled more by panic: seizing the king because he feared that the Woodvilles would take apart his vast estate, much of it built on dubious land transactions, and then, once he had attacked them, fearing a Woodville revanche when Edward came of age.

Perhaps also, having always been the perfect underling to his brother, he found the responsibility of being on his own too much for him. The timing and unexpectedness of Edward IV's death, the vacuum created by the sudden loss of his wide-ranging and very personal authority, and Richard's acute failure of judgement, combined to open the way for the first Tudor to become king, something that seemed wildly improbable up to that moment.

And with the Tudors came many things that might not have been otherwise. There was rule that was in many ways no more effective than Edward's but much more obviously disciplinarian. There were further implications for Britain. Wales, the Tudors' own country of origin, was already very much integrated and pacified, and Edward IV had increased the pace of this process. But Scotland remained – and was to remain – a troublesome land for England, and it was the marriage of Henry VII's daughter, Margaret, to the king of Scotland that was to lead to the eventual union of the two crowns under James I. Ireland had been much neglected by late medieval kings, who had France, Scotland and sometimes their own survival more in mind, and Henry VII was to initiate the more aggressive tactics that his successors followed, not necessarily with beneficial results.

Above all, if there had been no Henry VIII, would there have been the break from Rome and everything else that followed?

OTHER KEY DATES IN THIS PERIOD

1450 **Crisis over the loss of Normandy.** France had the upper hand in the Hundred Years War in the mid-fifteenth century. The loss of Normandy as an English possession in 1449 caused an acute political crisis. In February 1450 an unruly Parliament impeached Henry VI's chief minister. Through 1450 there was extended and widespread unrest among the lower classes aimed at the government. This became outright revolt in July, with Cade's Rebellion, centred on Kent, when the rebels took control of London for several days.

1453 **End of the Hundred Years War.** On 17 July the English defeat at the battle of Castillon put an end to centuries-old English rule in Aquitaine and to the last vestiges of English rule in France, apart from Calais and a small enclave around it. This was the effective end of the Hundred Years War. It was hearing the news of this defeat in August that allegedly caused Henry VI to lose his reason for nearly eighteen months.

1455 **Beginning of the Wars of the Roses.** The first battle of St Albans on 22 May was the start of the Wars of the Roses. Royal forces confronted the army of the duke of York in what was little more than a skirmish. The Yorkist victory gave the duke control of Henry VI – who, though recovered from madness, was now only a figurehead king – and enabled York to direct government until he lost power to the queen, Margaret of Anjou, in mid-1456.

1461 **Accession of Edward IV.** York, having returned from exile to claim the throne in 1460, had been defeated and killed by royalist forces at the battle of Wakefield. His son Edward took up his father's cause, defeated the Lancastrians at Mortimer's Cross in Wales, entered London and on 4 March proclaimed himself king, making good his claim by a great victory on 29 March over the Lancastrians at Towton in Yorkshire.

1470 **Brief return of Henry VI.** Warwick and Clarence (Edward IV's own brother), having fled to France after an abortive rebellion, and there made peace with Margaret of Anjou and her son, Prince Edward, returned, restoring Henry VI to the throne in October. Edward IV escaped but returned in March 1471, reclaiming his throne. Warwick was killed at Barnet in April, and invading Lancastrian forces were defeated at Tewkesbury in May and Prince Edward was killed. Edward IV ordered Henry VI's murder.

1478 **Death of Clarence**. Clarence had deserted Warwick on Edward's return from exile and had been pardoned but remained troublesome. In 1471–4 he quarrelled with Gloucester over the Warwick inheritance. He was a destabilizing influence in the regions where he was most powerful and there were rumours of treason. In 1478 he was condemned in Parliament and subsequently killed in the Tower, allegedly drowned in a butt of malmsey. His destruction indicates Edward's dominance and ruthlessness at this time.

1482 **Recovery of Berwick**. This key frontier town had been surrendered to the Scots in early 1461 in the last throes of Henry VI's rule. Anglo-Scottish relations were largely peaceable under Edward IV, once Scotland gave up supporting Lancastrians in exile. However, in 1482, encouraged by a disaffected Scottish noble, the duke of Albany, an expedition to Scotland was launched under Gloucester. It achieved little, but did retake Berwick.

1485 **Battle of Bosworth**. With French subvention and the support of Yorkist exiles, Henry Tudor landed at Milford Haven in Wales in August. He travelled through the midlands, gathering support. Richard III's forces, mustered at Nottingham, met Henry's at Market Bosworth near Leicester on 22 August. Some of Richard's greatest noble supporters failed to fight for him. Launching a brave, or foolhardy, attack on Henry's centre, Richard was killed, leaving the victorious Henry to claim the throne.

1495 **Poynings' Law**. Support in Ireland for the Yorkist pretender, Perkin Warbeck, and feuding among the Irish lords led Henry VII to intensify his rule there. In 1494 he sent a close servant, Sir Edward Poynings, to restore order and allegiance. A number of acts concerning the government of Ireland were passed in the Irish Parliament of 1494–5, including 'Poynings' Law', which severely curtailed the independence of the Irish Parliament from interference by the English king and council.

1534

Henry VIII tries to take control of Britain

JOHN GUY

Few events in England have rippled out to create a tsunami affecting the whole of the British Isles as much as those of 1534. In this year Henry VIII, who had divorced Katherine of Aragon and married Anne Boleyn, completed his break with the pope by getting Parliament to acknowledge him as Supreme Head in Earth of the Church of England. This meant that Henry had the right to appoint the bishops, vet the articles of faith and impose his will on the monasteries, all of which he did. To enforce his new powers, Henry revised and extended the treason law. Anyone disputing the royal supremacy, even by words alone, would be put on trial. To winkle out opposition, he set a test: an oath of supremacy and allegiance to the king and the 'imperial crown', to be taken by those holding offices in Church and State, sitting in Parliament, or who were in religious orders until he dissolved them.

Historians like to debate whether Henry ushered in a reign of terror, but this misses the bigger picture. The effects were not just confined to England. To justify his actions, Henry announced a new theory of kingship based on biblical and classical prototypes, giving an extra layer of meaning to the phrase the 'imperial crown'. In a nutshell, he claimed imperium (empire) with expansionist territorial overtones. When the duke of Norfolk discussed this with a bemused Spanish ambassador, he cited the precedent of King Arthur, 'emperor of Britain, Gaul, Germany and Thrace'. The ambassador could barely keep a straight face, saying it was a pity that Arthur hadn't also been 'emperor of Asia'.

Soon no one was laughing. In 1534, Henry began a radical overhaul of provincial government. Implemented in its initial stages by Thomas Cromwell, its focus was Wales, Ireland, the northern borderlands, and finally Scotland. All but Scotland were Tudor dominions, although more in name than in fact. The crown's writ ran unevenly north of the river Trent and was ignored in Wales and Gaelic Ireland: the people who really mattered in the outlying regions were the territorial magnates.

Scotland was, of course, an independent kingdom ruled by the Stewart king, James V, except that he was Henry VIII's nephew. This encouraged Henry to believe in Scotland's dynastic dependency, awakening dreams of Anglo-Scottish union. Earlier in his reign, Henry had revived Edward I's claim to be 'superior' and 'overlord' of Scotland. In and after 1534, he believed that Wales, Ireland and (increasingly) Scotland were 'within the orb of the "imperial crown" of England'.

No grand theory of state formation underpinned Henry's policy. He acted mainly out of fear. The northern border was a constant problem: it was vaguely defined and thieves crossed to and fro. Local magnates such as the Cliffords, Dacres or Percys kept the peace, but held their posts almost on a hereditary basis and were regarded by some as fifth columnists. While such criticism was often unfair, Henry was listening to their enemies. He especially questioned the loyalty of Lord Dacre of Gilsland, against whom charges of treason had been made.

A paranoid Henry came to believe that a group of nobles was plotting to overthrow him. Ireland posed the greatest threat, since outside the Pale (the area around Dublin where English rule was concentrated), the Gaelic lords were Catholics who refused to pay taxes or abandon Brehon law or customs (whereby disputes were arbitrated by Gaelic judges, the Brehons). Hitherto, their loyalty was secured by delegating royal power to a trusted magnate family: the Fitzgeralds, earls of Kildare. By combining a sufficient following in the Pale with their power in the Gaelic community, they had performed a juggling act that had kept Ireland stable for almost thirty years.

Wales was closer and the gentry more malleable, but still dangerous. English law was disregarded in the principality and border marcher lordships, where conflicts of jurisdiction enabled suspects to flee from one lordship to another. Jurors could easily be corrupted, and guns had been fired into the courts. Henry regarded Wales as a haven for insurgents. He was the more concerned because Welsh levies and horses formed the backbone of the royal army, and the favoured route for transporting troops to Ireland was through the (then) port of Chester. In 1534, Henry pounced on Lord Dacre and the Fitzgeralds in a pincer movement. Dacre was put on trial for treason and surprisingly found not guilty, the only nobleman to be acquitted by his peers during the reign. This did not deter Henry. As soon as Dacre walked free, he was re-arrested and returned to the Tower. He paid an astronomical fine of £10,000 and undertook not to go more than ten miles from London without the king's written permission.

By then, Henry had the ninth earl of Kildare in custody, intending to charge him with treason, but his detention sparked a spectacular revolt. Thomas Fitzgerald, Lord Offaly ('Silken Thomas'), the earl's heir, denounced Henry as a heretic and ordered those born in England to leave Ireland on pain of death. He threatened to ally with the pope and the king of Spain, and claimed that 12,000 Catholic troops were on their way to Ireland. Soon the country was convulsed: Dublin Castle was besieged and the rebels went on an orgy of looting and burning, terrifying the citizens. It took a huge army until August 1535 to suppress the revolt, costing 1,500 English lives and £40,000. Henry executed the ringleaders, but their revolt had turned the struggle into something approaching a Gaelic war of independence, committing him to a costly interventionist policy of 'Anglicizing' Ireland. This explains why, in 1541, he altered his official style from 'lord' to 'king' of Ireland. He was incensed by Irish taunts that his 'regal estate' there was granted by the pope, referring to Adrian VII's bull *Laudabiliter*, which had granted lordship over Ireland to the Anglo-Normans and implied that Henry held Ireland as a papal fiefdom.

In Scotland, Henry meant to prevent James V from allying with Spain or France, if those alliances meant Scotland continuing to support the pope. Opponents of the divorce from Katherine of Aragon had already fled across the border. So had James Griffydd ap Powell, a silver-tongued Welsh rebel who had talked his way out of the Tower of London promising to buy horses in Ireland for Anne Boleyn. Instead, he fled to Scotland, where he asked James V to aid a Welsh uprising against Henry.

Henry was angry with James for allowing Scots to join the Irish revolt. In 1534, he knew he could not fight on two fronts, so he tried conciliation. He admitted his nephew to the Order of the Garter and sent him a letter justifying his theory of kingship and royal supremacy. When James ignored it, Henry switched to threats, provoking James into his own 'imperial' claims and marriage to a French princess in 1537. When she died, James quickly chose another, Mary of Guise. Thereafter, Henry's determination to conquer Scotland by fair means or foul preoccupied him until his death.

In 1534, Cromwell sent a taskforce into Wales with orders to root out 'papists' and try treasons and felonies using English law. His efforts culminated in Acts of Union of 1536 and 1543 that assimilated the medieval principality and marcher lordships into twelve shires subject to English common law, complete with parliamentary representation at Westminster and a legal system modelled on the English assizes.

Henry VIII's vision of 'imperial' kingship meant that royal ecclesiastical supremacy was closely linked to an expansionist, centralizing impetus throughout the territories of the British Isles and Ireland – a highly explosive cocktail. In the longer term, the Reformation largely succeeded in England and Wales, whereas in Ireland the extirpation of Catholicism was always unrealistic. Tudor policy in Gaelic Ireland became identified with conquest and colonization, whereas in Wales the gentry traded their cooperation for patronage. In Scotland, there was a Reformation but no royal supremacy: when eventually the Presbyterian Kirk came into conflict with the Anglican ecclesiastical supremacy, the results could trigger sectarianism almost as bitter as that between Catholics and Protestants. Even in the minds of anglophile Scots, England's royal supremacy was a fundamental obstacle to union.

While Thomas Cromwell's taskforce was busy in Wales, its members travelled to Chester. At five o'clock in the morning of 15 September 1534, an earthquake shook the castle, which 'rocked like a cradle, to the great fear of us all therein'. This seismic event, creating panic as far away as Shrewsbury, might well be a metaphor for the half-century. When Henry VIII attempted to govern the outlying regions by a centralized system of command and control from Westminster, he bit off more than he could chew. He shoulders a large share of responsibility for what historians call the 'British' or 'Three Kingdoms' problem: the dilemma faced when the actions of political elites in one or two of these kingdoms trigger a hostile reaction in another, or when cross-border (especially religious) alliances could subvert or defeat crown policy. A major theme until the twentieth century, the problem lingers on in contemporary debates about 'Britishness', the future of Northern Ireland, and Scottish and Welsh devolution.

OTHER KEY DATES IN THIS PERIOD

1509 **Accession of Henry VIII**. Henry began his reign by courting popularity. He imprisoned Richard Empson and Edmund Dudley, ministers and debt collectors for Henry VII, for a year before executing them. Henry VIII promised full redress of subjects' grievances, but carried on almost exactly as his father had done. He would need even more money to pay for wars and new palaces, and to finance his dreams of conquests in France and Scotland. No attention was paid to Ireland.

1515 **Wolsey made lord chancellor**. Henry's first minister was Thomas Wolsey, who had risen to power as supremo for military procurement. Wolsey used Church patronage to climb the ladder, but the key to his success was his seeming ability to achieve everything that Henry desired. He was the first to experiment with the printing press for government forms and propaganda. He would diagnose the need for reforms in Ireland, but reverted to supporting the Fitzgeralds when his attempts failed.

1517 **Bad outbreak of 'the sweat'**. A viral pulmonary disease swept through the land on a terrifying scale. The symptoms were myalgia and headache, leading to abdominal pain, vomiting, unbearable headache and delirium, followed by cardiac palpitation, paralysis and death, all in under twenty-four hours. Henry VIII fled to the countryside. Ten thousand people died of it during the year, including 400 Oxford students in a week. The first outbreak had been in 1485, the last was in 1551.

1520 **The Field of Cloth of Gold**. Wolsey organized a meeting between Henry VIII and Francis I of France in search of a 'universal peace'. Held just outside Calais, the kings talked to little lasting effect. The event was mostly about magnificent displays of power and wealth. The English built a temporary palace crammed with artworks, with fountains dispensing free wine or beer. The main activities were dancing, banqueting, and a full-scale tournament. Francis beat Henry at wrestling.

1527 **The divorce comes into the open.** Henry VIII wanted to divorce Katherine of Aragon so he could marry Anne Boleyn; he was in love and wanted a legitimate male heir. Wolsey had to fix it, but Pope Clement VII was a virtual prisoner of Charles V, Katherine of Aragon's nephew, and refused to give dispensation. Wolsey's position was further eroded by a rebellion in East Anglia caused by his foreign policy, and Henry increasingly took charge.

1536 **Pilgrimage of Grace.** Anne Boleyn was executed for alleged adultery and incest. Cromwell started dissolving the monasteries and issuing articles and injunctions for the new Church of England. He triggered a massive revolt in Lincolnshire and the north. Forty thousand rebels wore pilgrim badges to show they were loyal to the Catholic faith and supported the monasteries. They would be brutally dispersed, but Cromwell was fatally undermined.

1542 **Battle of Solway Moss.** Henry's army defeated the Scots at the battle of Solway Moss. James V died shortly afterwards. His daughter, Mary Stewart, was queen at six days old; her mother, Mary of Guise, acted skilfully to protect her. Henry VIII was determined to betroth Mary Stewart to Prince Edward, his young son by Jane Seymour. When the Scots frustrated his efforts, he would invade Scotland, poisoning Anglo-Scottish relations.

1549 **Overthrow of Protector Somerset.** When Henry VIII died, his son Edward VI was 9 years old. For two years, Edward Seymour, duke of Somerset, was in charge. He too tried to conquer Scotland, but failed. Meanwhile, his push towards full-blooded Protestantism, currency debasements and inept social and economic reforms caused chaos. Mass protests in East Anglia were the closest thing to a Tudor class war. Somerset was overthrown, and the duke of Northumberland restored stability.

1588

The Armada is repelled

PAULINE CROFT

England was overshadowed by France and Spain in the mid-sixteenth century, but since the latters were usually at odds with each other, it could pursue its own interests safe from attack. Until 1550, England and Scotland were often at war, and for a while the marriage of Mary Queen of Scots to the son of Henri II threatened England with a Franco-Scottish 'pincer movement' on the Borders and in the Channel. However after the mid-century, France fell victim to a series of civil wars, largely the consequences of the Reformation. Spain was hardly touched by the Reformation and grew wealthy on profits from its New World territories. In England, Elizabeth and her council had to ensure religious divisions did not destabilize the country, and that Spain, the superpower, was kept at arm's length.

After the accession of Queen Elizabeth in 1558, friction between England and Catholic Spain became endemic. In 1580, the English sea captain Sir Francis Drake returned from his successful circumnavigation of the globe, including sailing up the Pacific coastline of South America and ransacking Spanish settlements. At the same time, Philip II of Spain's forces invaded Portugal, where the royal line

had died out, leaving Philip as the nearest heir. The conquest of Portugal brought huge extra colonial territories to
the Spanish crown; it also brought the deep-water Atlantic
port of Lisbon, a great naval asset. The successful takeover
of the Portuguese islands of the Azores and Terceira in
1582/3 confirmed Spain's new status as an oceanic power.

Meanwhile, France was devastated by divisions between
the Huguenot (Protestant) party and the extreme Catholic League. The death in 1584 of the duke of Anjou, next
in line to his childless brother Henri III, indicated that
the throne would go to their distant cousin, the Huguenot Henri of Navarre. That was intolerable not only to
the Catholic League but also to Philip II. They secretly
concluded an agreement that Spain would support the
League when civil war inevitably resumed. In the Netherlands – a dominion inherited by Philip from his father
– a longstanding rebellion appeared to be waning. Philip's
nephew, the prince of Parma, was proving an effective
general and in July 1584 the rebels' charismatic leader,
William the Silent, prince of Orange, was assassinated.

England now faced the possibility that Spain might
soon control the entire coastline of western Europe, from
the western Mediterranean around France to the borders
of north Holland. In August 1585, convinced she had no
other option, Elizabeth concluded the Treaty of Nonsuch,
sending aid to the Dutch. To Philip, that made England a
hostile power, and in October he began to think seriously
of an invasion. By spring 1587, preparations were proceed-
ing rapidly in Cadiz, the Basque ports and Lisbon. Then
in April, with no warning, Sir Francis Drake descended
on Cadiz and destroyed twenty-four ships, together with
considerable stores of food and munitions. From then on,
Spain was committed to the Enterprise of England.

There are four main points about the events of 1588.
First, despite Drake's raid, the scale of the Spanish action

was enormous, and twin-pronged. The Armada intended to link up with Parma's army of Flanders, which would punch home the invasion. On the vessels were 19,000 troops, almost all Spanish veterans. A further 27,000 were being readied by Parma for bringing across the Channel in requisitioned vessels and barges. The admiral, Medina Sidonia, commanded around 130 ships with the combined firepower of 360 guns. The campaign cost 45,000 ducats a day and tied down the whole military and naval resources of the Iberian peninsula, gravely affecting the defence of other parts of the Spanish monarchy. All that stood between England and defeat was the navy.

Second, despite the sheer size of the Armada, the contest was not completely unequal. Largely constructed in the 1570s, the English navy's 'race-built' vessels were fast, heavily armed and weatherly. They proved far more manoeuvrable than anything in the Spanish fleet, which never managed to implement its plan of grappling and boarding them. The English onboard, unlike the Spanish, were all skilled seamen and even the aristocrats in command, men like Lord Admiral Howard of Effingham and Lord Henry Seymour, all had some sailing experience and joined in the crews' labours. The royal navy consisted of thirty-six fighting ships with six smaller pinnaces, essentially message ships. They were backed up by 143 merchant vessels, some of them heavily gunned for privateering – preying on the enemy's shipping to make money out of captures. The best of the fleet, especially the ten biggest race-built vessels, was superb, but it was a small force to hold off the massive crescent-shaped formation coming up the Channel.

Third, the situation was rendered even more dangerous since the English privy council misread Spanish intentions and ordered troops to gather at Tilbury in Essex. Medina Sidonia intended to land his formidable forces in Kent.

He would establish a base for Parma's men, then, as soon as they were streaming across the Channel, the veterans carried on the Armada would storm to London. However, English strategy was superior to Philip's over-ambitious plan of linking up Medina Sidonia's fleet with Parma's army.

English land forces were in the wrong place, but the navy was not, for Drake had correctly divined Spanish intentions. The English ships initially tried to engage the Armada in Atlantic waters, but failed and returned to Plymouth. There, on 30 July 1588, over a hundred ships assembled in Plymouth Sound. Under cover of darkness, they skilfully tacked across the face of the oncoming Armada and round its southern tip. Advantageously placed upwind of their opponents, English vessels continually harassed the Spanish formation as it sailed eastwards.

Parma could not move his men safely across the Channel until the Armada had cleared it of English warships. He also faced a threat from rebel Dutch vessels trying to blockade him in, ready to fire on his unarmed barges if they put to sea. As long as the English navy remained capable of fighting, Parma's forces were unlikely to embark. Competently, Medina Sidonia brought most of his great fleet relatively unscathed into Calais Roads on 6 August, but the English still controlled the Channel.

The final point is that the English won the key battle. On the night of 7 August, eight fireships bore down on the Spanish galleons clustered off Calais. Faced suddenly with the burning vessels, most Spanish captains cut their anchors and fled. The Armada was transformed from a cohesive and still formidable fighting force to a scattering of panic-stricken vessels. Remarkably, they managed to regroup, but the following day, off Gravelines, the English came within artillery range and the battle raged for nine hours. Morale on the Armada was broken and Medina

Sidonia hanged a captain who disobeyed his orders to continue fighting. Twenty officers were arrested: a recent discovery in the Spanish archives has shown that even surrender was briefly considered.

Although the Armada sustained great damage, so far only six major galleons had been lost. Worse was to come on the way back; more than thirty ships, weakened by English guns, sank in severe storms off the west coasts of Scotland and Ireland. But, as the experienced admiral of the Biscayan squadron observed in his journal, the whole venture was lost when the English retained command of the Channel, preventing them from linking up with Parma. The ships went down as they were fleeing for home, long after their enterprise had ended in defeat.

There have been attempts, at the time and more recently, to argue that the outcome was just due to luck, or weather, or more in the nature of a draw, since Spain rebuilt a substantial navy in the early 1590s. Those arguments are unconvincing. The campaign of summer 1588 was an outstanding English victory. It was hard fought, and by the end, the English were almost out of ammunition. However, Drake's fireships were a brilliant tactical device and Gravelines must count as one of the greatest English naval actions. It is clear from the profusion of pamphlets across Europe that everyone accepted Spain had been resoundingly defeated. Philip II never again considered an invasion of England by combined sea and land forces: the best his rebuilt navy could do was to raid Cornwall.

The outcome of 1588 was a European turning point. England's successful resistance showed that Spain was not invincible, encouraging Protestants in the Netherlands and France to continue their struggle. The Dutch threw off Spanish rule and Henri of Navarre became king of France, bringing religious peace and economic recovery. The young James VI of Scotland, bound to England by the treaty of Berwick in 1586 but alienated by the execution of his mother Mary Queen of Scots in 1587, shrewdly seized the Armada moment to emphasise his claim as Elizabeth's heir. He wrote at the height of the crisis in summer 1588, assuring her of his support 'as your natural son and compatriot of your country'. In 1589 James also composed a 'Meditatioun' on the unity of 'the Ile of Britain', jointly protected by 'our virtewe' and God's 'michtie wind'. Scotland's king presented the events of 1588 as a victory for 'Britain' and for himself as the future first king of 'the Ile'. James had done little to help, but he recognised that the defeat of the Spanish Armada was already becoming a defining moment in the development of a national identity that would be both British and Protestant.

* * *

After 1588, the second part of Elizabeth's reign was darker, with England involved in continental wars and faced after 1594 with a gathering revolt in Ireland. The majority of the Irish population were still Gaelic in language and culture, and remained Catholic. Led by Hugh O'Neill, earl of Tyrone, they seized the chance of throwing off the English yoke, and hoped for Spanish aid. In England, a rising population put pressure on limited resources. Military costs led to heavy taxation and inflation; harvest failures and poor trade due to wartime disruption made life more difficult for most, and desperate for the poor. As the queen aged, there was concern over the succession. After the execution of Mary Queen of Scots in 1587, Mary's son James VI of Scotland was the most likely heir. Elizabeth never confirmed him as successor, but after 1586 she paid him a pension. On her death in March 1603, the new King James I was peacefully proclaimed by her privy council.

OTHER KEY DATES IN THIS PERIOD

1558 **Accession of Elizabeth.** Queen Mary had been a persecutor, burning over three hundred people at the stake for their beliefs. Her successor, her half-sister Elizabeth, was a moderate Protestant who hoped to avoid religious division by constructing a national Church acceptable to everybody. The Church of England never became completely comprehensive, but Elizabeth's mostly benign rule brought peace and security to England.

1560 **Scottish Reformation.** The absence of the half-French Mary Queen of Scots (who as wife of the heir to the French throne was at the French court) allowed a Protestant group to seize control. In 1560 they dominated the Scottish Parliament, abolishing the power of the papacy and the Mass. In England Sir William Cecil persuaded Elizabeth to use English troops to evict the French, who were forced to withdraw. The Protestants, initially a minority, steadily transformed Scotland into a Presbyterian country. This was crucial in developing Anglo-Scottish Protestant solidarity, allowing a sense of 'Britishness' slowly to emerge on both sides of the Border.

1570 **Rebellion and excommunication.** Northern England remained conservative in religion, and its leading nobles, the earls of Westmorland and Northumberland, joined a conspiracy in 1569: the duke of Norfolk would marry the widowed Mary Queen of Scots, a Catholic and Elizabeth's nearest heir, while the north would rise in rebellion. Just as the plot collapsed, the pope excommunicated Elizabeth, releasing her Catholic subjects from loyalty to her. This major tactical miscalculation made the plight of English Catholics more difficult.

1580 **Drake returns to England.** Drake left Plymouth in November 1577. Three years later, he returned, becoming only the second captain, and the first English one, to complete the circumnavigation of the globe. He brought with him booty from Spanish ships and settlements, so when the queen knighted Drake at Deptford on the deck of his weatherbeaten flagship *Golden Hind* she was condoning attacks on Philip II's subjects.

1596 **Oxfordshire Rising**. In November 1596, a few men gathered in western Oxfordshire to complain about recent enclosures. They plotted to throw down the fences enclosing new fields, to seize weapons from the houses of the gentry, perhaps even to murder some landowners. Two were executed, but the following year the privy council also rebuked the local gentry for their enclosures. The real problem was the disastrous series of four harvest failures from autumn 1594 to autumn 1597, which sent food prices soaring and hit the poor hardest.

1599 **The Globe Theatre**. Shakespeare was already established as a playwright, but in 1599 he and his troupe, the Lord Chamberlain's Men, moved into the Globe. They became the capital's leading company, performing among other great plays *The Merchant of Venice*, *Henry V*, *Julius Caesar* and *Hamlet*. Between 1570 and 1630, England produced a profusion of literary talent that has hardly ever been matched, with the Globe dominating the London scene.

1638

Scots revolt against Charles I

RAB HOUSTON

To appreciate the importance of 1638, we need to understand the diversity of British politics, religion and society in the early seventeenth century. England, Wales, Scotland and Ireland only became a unified monarchy in 1603 with the Union of the Crowns. Administratively, Wales and Ireland had been closely integrated into the English state since the time of Henry VIII. Scotland had its own Parliament, a separate legal and administrative system, a different currency, and a distinct Church of Scotland. The 1603 Union worked to secure the English succession and to reduce lawlessness on the Border. Yet there was always a legacy of what John Morrill calls 'distrust, double-dealing, broken promises, and betrayal'.

Understanding was limited by the diversity of the three kingdoms. England was firmly Protestant (less than 10 per cent were Catholics) as was Lowland Scotland; the Church of Ireland was Anglican, but most Irish people were Catholics, as were many in the Highlands and Islands of Scotland. Land ownership was widespread in England, but society was much more polarized in Scotland and Ireland. At least a third of the population of Scotland spoke only Gaelic, 90 per cent of Irish and a similar proportion of Welsh spoke only their native language. Few people had a direct political voice. Restricted to perhaps a quarter of adult Englishmen, the parliamentary franchise in Scotland was minuscule, but riots gave more opportunity for women, workers and the young to express themselves.

England and Wales was the wealthiest and most economically dynamic part of Britain. It had about five million people, Ireland just over a million and Scotland somewhere between eight and nine hundred thousand. Most lived in the countryside: 10 per cent of English people lived in towns of 5,000 or more, but just 3 per cent of Scots and 1 per cent of Irish were urban dwellers. Men married for the first time at about 26, women at 23 and a third of marriages were remarriages caused by a partner's death. Life was short. Diseases like plague and typhus, over which people had almost no control, could kill thousands; one child in five born alive was dead by its first birthday. This was a violent society, which saw the highest rate of capital punishment in recorded British history.

* * *

Crowned king of England in 1625, Charles I progressed north for his coronation as king of Scots in 1633. On his visit, he basked in the compliance of Scotland's still separate Parliament and the utter obedience of his instruments of government in Scotland – privy council, Church and court. His power within the multiple monarchy of Britain and Ireland, newly made at the accession of his father James I in 1603, seemed absolute. Yet, just five years later, Scotland was convulsed by a revolution that caused monarchical authority to evaporate throughout the three kingdoms of England (with Wales), Scotland and Ireland,

and eventually led to Charles' execution in 1649. Intelligent, flexible yet tenacious, James proved a much better king of Scotland than of England, but he was able to keep all his kingdoms together – and apart. His second son, Charles, proved to be good at neither.

At the heart of Charles I's failure was the close link between religion and politics. Europe's Renaissance princes had grown politically powerful – too potent for many subjects. They feared monarchs were ready to use the authority they had by virtue of simply being princes ('prerogative' powers) to establish arbitrary or 'absolute' government untrammelled by representative institutions such as England's Parliament or the rule of law. Rulers also preferred their subjects to follow their religion. James was a Protestant, but not a Calvinist. Charles was thought to be a closet Catholic and was married to an open one, Henrietta Maria.

To a modern reader, dislike of 'big government' may be understandable, but religious affiliation seems a personal choice. In the seventeenth century religion had very public implications, especially for a monarch, because princes ruled as well as reigned. To contemporaries faced with the last great war of religion on the Continent, the Thirty Years War (1618–48), and the real threat of the extirpation of Protestantism, Catholicism or 'popery' was viewed as a danger not only to faith, but also to all rights, liberties, property and privileges enjoyed by British Protestants. Catholics were seen as an early modern fifth column, forever ready to plot and implement treason. More specifically, William Laud, archbishop of Canterbury since 1633, introduced religious changes around a Catholic-leaning doctrine known as Laudianism that emphasized ceremony in church and what he called 'the beauty of holiness'.

Charles' desire for a more traditional and visually reverent Church encountered opposition, though English people worried more about the purely political side of his policies as he tried to enforce 'absolutist' rule, dispensing with Parliament from 1629. His drive to extend his personal authority and dispense with what he saw as a penny-pinching and sometimes insolent Parliament went well in the 1630s. He used traditional means of raising money coupled with prerogative courts such as the High Commission, the supreme power in the Church under the crown, and the hated Star Chamber (a civil and criminal court) to curb religious and political opposition and force through questionable taxes. Discontent at his perceived tyranny was widespread in England at the end of 1637, yet he was riding high – as symbolized by Van Dyck's portrait of him in 1636. In spring 1638 Charles won an important test case, 'Hampden's Case', about the legality of one of his exactions, 'ship money', and looked set to continue pursuing his vision of divine right absolutist monarchy.

It was Scotland that brought his ambitions crashing down. The religious reaction there was both stronger and swifter than in England because the Scottish Reformation had followed a more radical trajectory. English Protestantism was a relatively mild creed, albeit with a more militant, 'Puritan' wing that aimed to push forward its vision of a godly kingdom on earth. Scottish Calvinists were made of sterner stuff, basing their Reformation on a strict version of Protestantism and a 'Presbyterian' form of church government that involved chosen laymen as well as the parish clergy in decision making.

Scots disliked and did all they could to subvert and bypass the Episcopalian church order imposed across Britain by James I. Charles' government in Scotland was less popular than it had been in 1633 – but not irrevocably so – when he had the Scottish bishops and Laud draw up a Book of Common Prayer for Scotland in 1637. Anti-Calvinist, its attempted introduction acted as a catalyst to the organization of petitions against what was seen as arbitrary rule, as well as a series of riots, the most famous in July 1637 at St Giles Kirk, Edinburgh.

Charles at first saw the opposition as a little local difficulty, but in February 1638 a group of nobles, magistrates and clergy signed a National Covenant in Edinburgh. On the face of it, this simply bound together like-minded Presbyterians protecting their religion – written by and for people who wished to unite in a special relationship with God. But it went further. Striking at the heart of Charles' government, it asserted the primacy of the law, the Presbyterian Church and true reformed faith (Calvinism) over royal prerogative, episcopacy and crypto-Catholicism.

During summer 1638 the marquis of Hamilton acted as Charles' commissioner or viceroy in Scotland and in the autumn both the Scottish Parliament and the first General Assembly of the Church of Scotland since 1617 were called. Hamilton hoped these representative bodies could be used to legitimate a measured introduction of liturgical reform and thus restore royal authority. In fact, they were dominated by Presbyterian clergy and pro-Covenant nobles and together they swept away the royal supremacy over Church, bishops, the Court of High Commission and the Prayer Book.

Too late, Charles was swayed by Thomas Wentworth, lord deputy of Ireland since 1632, who urged a strong line to bring the Scots to heel. Acutely aware of the seething discontent of the Irish, Wentworth believed (prophetically) that concessions in one of the three kingdoms would only provoke similar demands elsewhere. Charles raised an army to bring the Scots back to obedience, but its effect in the so-called Bishops' Wars of 1639–40 in Scotland was to destabilize further all the countries over which he ruled. Eventual defeat by the Scots alarmed the English Parliament, which blamed Charles for the unrest and tried to curb his powers of taxation and military command.

Failure in Scotland gave encouragement to opponents of absolutism and popery in England, first in withdrawing the grudging consensus in local government and taxation that had allowed the decentralized early Stuart state to function. Lacking a standing army or anything except the most rudimentary bureaucracy, Charles could only watch the obedience of his subjects drain away. The Scottish debacle also emboldened opponents of Charles' policies when he was obliged to call Parliament after eleven years of 'personal rule'. Amid mounting disquiet, the king was forced to flee London when rebellion broke out in Ireland in 1641. Military fortunes ebbed and flowed until the decisive defeat of the Royalists at Naseby in 1645. Charles, duplicitous as ever, tried to do a deal with the Scottish nobility, but that alliance too was defeated in 1648. Throughout the decade from 1638 the fortunes of all parts of Britain and Ireland were inextricably entwined.

Yet even at the end of 1638 cracks were beginning to appear in the Covenanting theocracy. In parts of Scotland, such as the north-east that would in the eighteenth century provide many supporters for the Jacobite cause, Episcopalianism was strong. The Covenanting movement meanwhile contained a fundamental tension between Presbyterians, whose main interest was in protecting their Calvinist Reformation, and the broader political drive to create a more limited monarchy. The later decision to try to confirm the Scottish Revolution by entering into the Solemn League and Covenant with English Parliamentarians in 1643 led to the fateful Scottish invasion of England. This openly divided the Covenanters and gave Charles the chance to try to divide and rule his Scottish enemies. However, the alliance remained unified long enough to defeat Charles, only to fragment irrevocably in 1647–8.

In short, the Scottish Revolution of 1638 both reflected and further encouraged a rising tide of sullen disobedience and active opposition that culminated in England with the calling of Parliament in 1640 and in Ireland with the rebellion of 1641 onwards. Charles realized too late both the strength of feeling against his political and religious policies and that the concessions he had made to the Scots struck at the basis of his authority. At the end of 1638 he had capitulated to a Scottish Revolution that nevertheless continued ruthlessly and relentlessly, by intrigue and force of arms, to dismantle the political and religious establishment his father had created in Scotland. 'Too weak to be absolute, too ambitious to be anything else', Charles' arrogant and inept religious policies squandered an inheritance of political stability and plunged not only his dynasty, but the monarchy itself, into crisis.

The English Civil Wars and interregnum that filled the years up to 1660 are unthinkable without the events in Scotland in 1638 that began what are known broadly as the Wars of the Three Kingdoms. The Scots began Charles' downfall and their Covenanting ideas set the tone for armed resistance throughout Britain in the following decade. It was a true watershed in *British* history. Above all, 1638 highlights the way that events in one part of Britain influenced the development of others and indeed of the whole United Kingdom. It exemplifies the need for a British rather than purely an English history of the 'north Atlantic archipelago' in the early modern period.

OTHER KEY DATES IN THIS PERIOD

1603 **Union of the crowns.** Elizabeth I never married, and without an heir her crown passed to the man whose mother, Mary Queen of Scots, she had allowed to be executed in 1587. King of Scots at just 13 months old after Mary was deposed by her own nobility in 1567, James VI inherited a much richer kingdom than his own and quickly moved to London, where he was crowned James I of England with 'silent joye, noe great shouting'.

1608 **Plantation of Ulster.** Following the shock of a rebellion by Sir Cahir O'Doherty of Inishowen, previously a loyal ally, James I adopted a radical scheme for systematically colonizing Ulster with English and Scottish Protestants, in the belief it would subdue unrest and win over the 'rude and barbarous Irish' to 'civility'. 100,000 Scots and 20,000 English settled in Ulster over the century, sowing the seeds of discontent among the indigenous population that are still evident in sectarian tensions today.

1609 **Statutes of Iona.** This was James' parallel response to his other problem area, the Gaelic-speaking, Catholic-leaning, clan society of the Highlands and Islands of Scotland. A coherent and ideologically driven attempt to alter the nature of the region, it represents an early form of ethnic cleansing of people who allegedly manifested 'grite crueltie and inhumane barbaritie'. The statutes struck at the heart of clan society, which was not principally about kinship, but about feasting and fighting.

1623 **Last English subsistence crisis.** While Scotland still had famines in the 1690s and beyond, and Ireland tragically until the 1840s, the last time large numbers of people died of hunger in England was at the end of James I's reign – and that mainly in the north-west. Thereafter England became the most agriculturally productive country in Europe and the one with the highest average standard of living, creating the preconditions for the eighteenth-century 'consumer revolution'.

1641 **Rebellion in Ireland.** Dispossessed and oppressed by the Plantation Protestants, native Irish Catholics rose in bloody rebellion, stirring up the fears of popish plots and threats of invasion that had haunted English people since the days of the Spanish Armada (1588) and Gunpowder Plot (1605). Extensive and prolonged, the rising permeated British politics during the 1640s and was not finally suppressed until Cromwell's arrival in Ireland in 1649.

1645–6 **Peak of English witchcraft executions.** While most English witchcraft accusations were very personal, Matthew Hopkins, Puritan, lawyer and self-proclaimed witch-finder general, single-handedly created the most intensive hunt for witches in English history: over a hundred women were executed. Witchcraft accusations show a mental world saturated by the supernatural.

1649 **Execution of Charles I.** Being a monarch had always been a dangerous occupation and plenty of previous English kings had died in battle or by assassination, but none had been judicially murdered by his own people. The death sent a shudder through the elites of early modern Europe. It also introduced a bold experiment in both social engineering and republican government that was reversed (but never forgotten) in 1660.

1662

Charles II pays a heavy price for his Restoration

JOHN MORRILL

In 1662, the peoples of England, Wales, Scotland and Ireland were coming to terms with the effects of twenty years of civil war and political and religious violence. In the course of the 1640s and 1650s, parish churches had been purged of all 'monuments of idolatry and superstition', Christmas and Easter were banned, the Prayer Book was proscribed, bishops, Church courts and trappings of hierarchy were swept away. A variety of religious sects sprang up with more (Baptist) or less (Quaker) state encouragement. In 1649 Charles I was put on trial and beheaded for treason against his people, and monarchy and the House of Lords were abolished. A godly army set up and then pulled down various constitutional experiments, the most long lasting of which made the Lord General Oliver Cromwell the lord protector.

The most contentious of Cromwell's achievements was the military subjugation of Ireland and Scotland. In Ireland, the Commonwealth governments took almost half the land from Catholics born in Ireland, and gave it to

Protestants from England. The population shrank by one-third. The proportion of British adult males who died as a result of the fighting was higher than in the First World War.

The revolutionaries made many enemies and few friends. By 1660, there was an overwhelming desire for Restoration – for a return to hereditary monarchy, to bishops and Cranmer's prayers, to Christmas pies, maypoles, sport on Sunday afternoons. But the Revolution cast a long shadow. There were enough supporters of the Puritan way – freedom of conscience, the imposition of strict moral codes, plain dealing and plain dress – for the celebration of old and new freer ways to cause political polarization. All kinds of enthusiasm were discredited. A new spirit of dispassionate, sceptical enquiry challenged the claims of all churches and churchmen. So Church and king were restored, but had to face their critics.

The alliance was fatally wounded by the fact that none of the three monarchs in this half-century was a supporter of the established Church. Charles II hid his private beliefs so deeply behind a protective chameleon coating (he was all things to all men) that historians are still not sure whether he was a secret Catholic or an early Deist. James II and VII was a Catholic with an extreme case of 'convertitis', and William III would do whatever was necessary to ensure that English politicians would underwrite his crusade against Louis XIV. And so the central instabilities of the Restoration, so evident in 1662, created crisis after crisis in 1672, 1679, 1688 and 1701.

It took Louis XIV of France, threatening to impose popery and arbitrary government on the country, to persuade the political elite to convert the country into a fiscal-military state capable of dominating Europe and claiming a lion's share of the world's commerce. That threat was an indirect result of the instabilities of the 1662 settlement, but without those, the trajectory of later seventeenth-century politics would have been very different.

* * *

The year 1662 was a warm, bright year: the warmest winter and spring of the whole half-century and one of the warmest overall – only dwarfed by the scorching summer of 1686. The scars of civil war, the buildings burned and wrecked by war, were being repaired and replaced. Carpenters and masons were reconverting churches from whitewashed auditoria into sacramental spaces; theatres were being built at an unprecedented rate. Samuel Pepys was able to see a new show most weeks, including *The Knight of the Burning Pestle, The French Dancing Master* and the first recorded Punch and Judy show. The king was to be seen at many of these plays with his pregnant mistress, a casual insult to the reformation of manners at the heart of Interregnum high-mindedness.

A grimmer kind of theatre was enacted at Tyburn, where the procession of regicides dragged there to be half-hanged, eviscerated and cut into pieces was completed. The Restoration made an example of those who took part in Charles I's trial and execution but passed a wide-ranging indemnity that protected everyone else from prosecution for what they had done over the past twenty years.

But a series of parliamentary acts revealed an ongoing neurosis: in late 1661 an Act 'against tumultuous petitioning' required all but the humblest petitions to be initiated by justices of the peace and grand juries at quarter sessions; the 1662 Licensing Act brought in a tougher regime for the control of the press than had existed even before the Revolution – one of its results was effectively to drive newspapers off the streets for most of the next thirty years. Later in 1662, an Act 'for the relief of the poor' allowed local officials to remove forcibly all newcomers from a parish if they were 'likely to be chargeable' to the poor rate and to return them to their previous place of residence. This was motivated as much by fear of sedition as of vagrancy.

For the better off, 1662 was a good year. The shops were full of goods, the king's wife introduced the English to tea and the Great Turk coffee house opened in London. In 1662 what Pepys called 'the college of virtuosos' (the Royal Society for the Improvement of Natural Knowledge) was established by royal charter, and its meetings were one of the few things to distract the king from pleasures of the chase (human and animal). In 1662, Isaac Newton was in his first year at Cambridge, but Christopher Wren was designing weather-clocks, and Robert Boyle was announcing his discovery about the inverse relationship of volume and pressure in gases. In Derby John Flamsteed, later to be the first astronomer royal, made his first-ever recording of the partial solar eclipse.

Internationally, 1662 was a quiet year. There was no European war, although the Chinese seized Formosa (Taiwan) from the Dutch. Charles II married Catherine of Braganza, a Portuguese princess on 3 May, bringing Bombay and Tangier as part of her dowry. To cover some of the costs of setting her up with an appropriate household, Charles sold Dunkirk, occupied by Cromwell's troops, back to France for £400,000.

In 1660, Charles II had made it clear that he wanted an inclusive settlement. He gave more office, more patronage and more financial rewards to his father's enemies than to his father's friends: his friends would not send him on his travels again. He attempted to achieve this breadth in both secular and religious affairs; but he succeeded only in the former. The forces of religious reaction were too strong for him, and in 1662, legislation was passed in each of his kingdoms privileging those who embraced the spirit of the Elizabethan and Jacobean settlements. In England, the 1662 Act of Uniformity restored a Church both Catholic and Reformed, which looked Catholic and sounded Protestant, with a prayer book little changed from that of Elizabeth, with lordly bishops in their medieval palaces.

Membership of this state Church was made mandatory, with fines and other minor penalties on those who would not attend; and with heavier penalties on those who tried to worship, even in private, according to their experience and conscience. For the next two hundred years, the position in English law was that only communicating members of the Church of England could hold public office, or attend university or an inn of court. Charles had wanted to loosen up the terms of membership of his national Church, believing persecution would breed far more sedition than tolerating separation would. But since he never relished a fight, and since his Parliament and many of his advisers were adamant that the Church needed to be true to its pre-war traditions and that tolerance would allow sedition to fester, he gave in.

As a result, more than one in ten of the clergy resigned, and a similar proportion of layfolk opted out of regular church attendance and into attendance at conventicles – meetings of dissenters for worship. This created a fundamental instability in English political culture: between those who believed that monarchy needed to be underpinned by a hierarchical, narrow, national Church; and those who wanted a different kind of national Church or no national Church at all. In time, these tensions congealed into the two great parties: Tory (strong Church equals strong monarchy equals security of life and property); and Whig (religious pluralism as a hallmark of personal liberty as a hallmark of economic and social prosperity).

Much the same happened in Scotland. A ruined nobility were more ruthless in reclaiming social power and happy to see the power of the Kirk broken and its ministers humbled, and a settlement made that was both erastian (advocating the doctrine of state supremacy over the Church in ecclesiastical affairs) and episcopalian (governed by bishops). The purge on the uncompromising led in 1662 to the expulsion of one third of the clergy. Such men remained convinced they were instruments of God's will; this made them more seditious than English dissenters. The more seditious they became, the more brutal the reactions of the Scottish establishment; a dark era of torture, massacre, assassination and fanaticism ensued. In 1689 the Revolution in Scotland was not to be the peaceful fudge that it was in England, but violent, counter-vindictive and partisan.

In Ireland, too, religion was the crunch issue. There was spasmodic persecution of Catholic clergy, but little attempt to compel ordinary Catholics to attend Protestant worship, let alone to convert them. But the big problem was land. In England and Scotland, compromises between the purchasers of confiscated land were usually possible (the purchasers of the land surrendering the title but staying on as tenants on low rents), but in Ireland the problem was unmanageable. More than 40 per cent of the land of Ireland had been confiscated and redistributed to those who had bankrolled English armies to put down the Irish rebellion of 1641 and to 30,000 soldiers who had effected the reconquest. In Ireland, unlike the king's other kingdoms, in 1662 those confiscations were deemed legal. Charles II promised in 1660 to restore those who had not been directly implicated in the massacres of 1641 and who had supported his lord lieutenant against the Parliamentarians. He also promised to compensate those who had to surrender land to that group.

These were unrealizable promises. In 1662, the Irish Act of Settlement set up a Court of Claims to examine all these issues. It was overwhelmed by the volume of work and lack of land to square the circle. It left almost everyone dissatisfied except those with family connection or clout with the Irish administration to get their claims to the head of the queue. The 80 per cent of the population who were Catholic were left with 20 per cent of the land. It left England with a permanent problem of garrisoning Ireland and facing a low-level insurgency of 'Tories' and 'Rapparees' (brigands). It ensured that the Revolution of 1688 in Ireland was not in the least Glorious. It was another bloodbath.

The year 1662 was a time of deceptive calm. Everywhere there is evidence that in the face of a grieving Puritan minority, the peoples of England and Wales, Scotland and Ireland set out to enjoy the pleasures forbidden them for twenty years, and engaged in febrile efforts to silence or intimidate those who might try to start the conflict all over again. Charles II talked of religious liberty but ordered the assassination of his most implacable opponents as they plotted against him in exile. The Puritan minister Adam Martindale gave up his pulpit in Rostherne, Cheshire, and invited his parishioners round on Sunday evenings to criticize the sermons given earlier in the day by his successor. He was one of many. What was not restored at the Restoration was peace of mind.

OTHER KEY DATES IN THIS PERIOD

1653 **Cromwell as lord protector**. Cromwell – wearied by the failure of the Rump Parliament to come up with a new constitution, a new religious framework and more social justice – used his troops to disband it (20 April) and established a Nominated Assembly of godly men with a mandate (4 July) to find long-term solutions. It failed completely and in December Cromwell reluctantly agreed to become lord protector under a constitution drawn up by General John Lambert.

1657 **Cromwell refuses the crown**. Cromwell was put under great parliamentary pressure to become king. Since the protectorate was not 'known to the laws', he had more discretionary power than many MPs thought wise; and they thought King Oliver would broaden his support among the many who admired monarchy but not the House of Stuart. But Cromwell's fear that because God had 'blasted the family and the name' it meant He did not want any monarch, made him decline.

1660 **Death of Puritanism**. After Cromwell's death in 1658, there was political meltdown and the army too fell into factions. In February George Monck, the general in charge of Scotland, marched south and ordered free elections. Parliament recalled the king, but even before they did so, Easter was celebrated in thousands of parishes, and maypoles sprang up on village greens; both were symbols that the Puritan experiment had failed.

1672 **Test Acts**. Charles went to war with the Dutch in alliance with the French but chickened out of a deal with Louis XIV to declare himself a Catholic. He did, however, attempt, by prerogative action, to give full rights of religious assembly to both Protestant and Catholic Dissenters. This backfired, however, and Parliament used the power of the purse to force Charles to accept new restrictions on practising Catholics (the Test Acts).

1679 **Failure of the Exclusion Bill.** Charles II had no legitimate children, and, as he aged, many Protestants feared both his authoritarianism (bribing of MPs, excessive use of discretionary power, closeness to Catholic France) and the prospect that he would be succeeded by his Catholic brother, James. The Whigs tried (but failed in the House of Lords) to break the hold of 'divine right theory' by promoting an Exclusion Bill, making Parliament the arbiter of the succession.

1685 **Accession of King James.** In February Charles was succeeded by James II and VII, who easily saw off rebellions in England by Charles' bastard son, the duke of Monmouth, and in Scotland by the rabidly Presbyterian earl of Argyll. Initially James tried to coax the Tory Anglicans into working with him to give equal rights to his Catholic co-religionists. They defied him.

1688 **Glorious Revolution.** By 1688, James was trying to work with Whigs and Dissenters to promote his Catholic cause. The birth of a Catholic heir and the sheer scale of his attack on Anglican privilege provoked a section of the elite to invite William of Orange to invade to protect Protestantism, the succession rights of his wife (James' daughter Mary) and to bring English arms and cash into the international coalition against Louis XIV.

1689 **William and Mary.** After James fled to France, there was vicious civil war in Ireland, political blood-letting in Scotland and a painful set of compromises in England that allowed William and Mary to rule jointly on terms that some at the time (and since) believed to have changed the nature of monarchy and which others denied. The most important change was the twenty-five years' war with France (1688–1713) that transformed the finances and governance of Britain.

1697 **Peace in Europe.** The Treaty of Ryswick brought a fragile peace to Europe, although everyone knew that a war between rival claimants to the Spanish succession was imminent. In Ireland, Parliament reneged on the promises that

William's generals had made to the Catholics and began a process of sectarian measures (the Penal Laws) that enshrined social and religious injustice. It was also the year St Paul's Cathedral (rebuilt after the Great Fire) reopened for business.

1745

The Jacobites rebel

DANIEL SZECHI

The British Isles on the eve of this momentous struggle was apparently politically stable and in no danger of violent upheaval. But beneath the façade of union and the increasingly visible integration of the Scottish and English economies there was a deep and enduring hostility to the prevailing order. England, Scotland and Ireland had for thirty years been ruled by the Whig party (the party primarily responsible for the revolution of 1688), while their old rivals, the Tories, sourly did what they could to oppose them through conventional politics. A radical element within the Tories' ranks (the Jacobites), however, went much further and plotted and dreamed of restoring the heirs of James II and VII, the Stuart Catholic king driven out by the revolution.

The Tory party's first loyalty was to the Church of England, and the Jacobites among them inclined to the exiled Stuart dynasty because they feared the Hanoverian dynasty's apparent religious indifference was undermining the Anglican hold on society and hence the three kingdoms' special relationship with God.

In Scotland, where the Union had as yet failed to deliver

the economic uplift that had been promised in 1707, ongoing political and economic fusion with England remained a bitter source of division and resentment. So, when the Jacobites emerged as the champions of national independence, a wide swath of Scottish society was immediately drawn to them.

In Ireland the Catholic majority was systematically discriminated against economically, socially and legally by the Whig regime, and for two generations thousands of young Irish Catholic men had been slipping away to the Continent to serve in the armies of France and Spain. There they openly maintained their allegiance to the Stuarts and did what they could to further the Jacobite cause, while those in Ireland secretly yearned for news of the Stuart 'attempt' they hoped would liberate them from Whig oppression.

The Jacobite uprising that began in July 1745 came, too, in the midst of Britain's first major conflict in nearly twenty years. The War of Austrian Succession began in 1740 when Frederick the Great of Prussia invaded Silesia, and Britain threw in its lot with the beleaguered Empress Maria-Theresa against Frederick's principal ally: France. And though Britain had done tolerably well in the opening stages of the conflict, by 1745 things had taken a turn for the worse. Maria-Theresa's armies were hard-pressed by Prussian, French and Spanish attacks, and Britain's ally, the Netherlands, was flagging and war-weary. Worse still, Britain's main army, led by George II's youngest son, William Augustus, duke of Cumberland, was defeated at the battle of Fontenoy in modern Belgium on 11 May 1745. This, in many respects, acted as the trigger for the Jacobite rebellion.

* * *

Prince Charles Edward Stuart ('Bonny Prince Charley'), grandson of James II and VII, had been summoned to France in December 1743 to head a French invasion of southern England scheduled to take place in early 1744. Bad weather, the royal navy and English Tory faintheartedness eventually brought that attempt to naught, and the prince frustratedly idled away his time for the next year. Or so it appeared. In fact, with the help of a syndicate of Irish merchants resident in France, he was secretly preparing a surprise attack on the British Isles. The news of the English defeat at Fontenoy provided exactly the opening he needed. On 5 July Charles Edward sailed from Nantes with two ships. His plan was to force the Jacobites of the British Isles to live up to their promises by throwing himself into their midst. If enough Jacobites responded and he could expose the weakness – as he believed – of the Whig regime he was sure the French would invade and victory would be his.

It was either a bold gambit or a foolhardy gamble, and certainly the odds against success were greatly increased when the prince encountered a royal navy patrol on the way to Scotland and one of his ships was damaged and forced to turn back (with most of his painfully accumulated arms, ammunition and a body of Irish soldiers aboard). Charles Edward thus arrived at Arisaig in Scotland on 25 July accompanied by few more than the famous 'seven men of Moidart'.

Once ashore, however, Charles Edward worked wonders. Bluntly told to go home by one appalled Highland chieftain, Charles smoothly countered, 'I am come home.' Within three weeks his legendary charm had persuaded two senior clan chieftains to support the rising and other Jacobites were stirring throughout Scotland. As his little army of about 1,500 marched south from Glenfinnan on 19 August it steadily accumulated men. Many were doubtless forced out by their landlords and feudal superiors, but others certainly joined to support the cause that Charles Edward represented.

Hard marching and adept manoeuvring soon put the government's army in Scotland, commanded by Sir John Cope, at a disadvantage it could only reverse by retreating. Luck and judgement then combined to allow the now 2,500-strong Jacobite army to seize Edinburgh on 17 September and defeat Cope at the battle of Prestonpans on 21 September. In little more than a month the Jacobites had virtually won control of Scotland. The only question was what to do next. Charles Edward had no doubts: he passionately advocated a march on London as hard and fast as the march on Edinburgh. His Scottish senior officers were not so sure, and only agreed when the prince assured them he had firm pledges of an English Jacobite rising if they would only march into England.

The 4,500-man Jacobite army accordingly crossed the border on 8 November and rapidly progressed south-wards, as far as Derby by 4 December, capturing Carlisle and Manchester en route and outmanoeuvring two more government armies to put itself in a position where it could strike unmolested at London. But by the time they reached Derby, Charles Edward's officers were questioning the whole enterprise. Bar a handful of militants recruited in Manchester, the English Jacobites had conspicuously failed to materialize. Charles Edward's only solution to the predicament was to urge that the army press on and attack London, a city of approximately 500,000 people. At a council of the senior officers on 5 December the prince was outvoted by a coterie of officers centred on his most able commander, Lord George Murray. Instead, the Jacobite army was to retreat. Ironically, unbeknown to any of those involved, this decision was taken just as financial panic paralysed the City of London and the French army and navy were in the final stages of throwing together the invasion the Jacobites so desperately needed.

Regardless, the retreat was conducted with great skill. Murray dodged and feinted his way past the pursuing government armies, and by Christmas 1745 the rebels were back in Scotland, resting and re-equipping in Glasgow. Government pressure on the Jacobites now became relentless, however. William Augustus, duke of Cumberland and commander-in-chief of the British army, had been called back from the Netherlands with the best British regiments. All across England and Wales Whig loyalists were raising money, forming volunteer units and enlisting in the army to fight in defence of Protestantism and liberty (as they saw it). The royal navy was doing its best to isolate Scotland from the Continent, and Scottish Whigs led by the earl of Loudon were gathering an army of their own in northern Scotland.

Even so, the first government attempt to challenge the Jacobites' control of central Scotland, led by General Henry ('Hangman') Hawley, was handily defeated by a revitalized, 8,000-strong Jacobite army at Falkirk on 17 January 1746. The victory was, though, a hollow one. The threat to their homes and families posed by Loudon's army in northern Scotland united a majority of Charles Edward's officers in demanding a further retreat northwards, which only ended when the tired army reached Inverness on 18 February.

The struggle was, however, far from over. For the next two months the Jacobites raided and probed south from Inverness, and Cumberland's army raided and probed north from Aberdeen. Both sides were gathering their strength for the final crisis. This came when, for the first time, Cumberland succeeded in surprising the Jacobites by marching north in early April while nearly half their army was away from Inverness raiding and recruiting. He consequently caught the Jacobites at a severe disadvantage when he confronted them on Drummossie Moor near Culloden House on 16 April.

The ensuing battle did not take long. The Jacobites attacked in traditional Highland style (though many of the men in their ranks were in fact Lowlanders), but over ground that did not favour the headlong charge that was its culmination. Cumberland's carefully deployed infantry and artillery were thus able to use their superior firepower to maximum effect. Within little more than an hour over a third of the 4,000 or so Jacobites on the field were dead or wounded and the rest in were flight. Charles Edward was hustled away in tears before the government cavalry could capture him. According to tradition, as he left, one of his senior officers Lord Elcho, overwhelmed by the death of his friends and the ruin of the Scottish Jacobite cause, shouted after him, 'Run, you cowardly Italian!' Hardly fair, but a token of what was to come.

Charles Edward fled into the Highlands, where he refused to sanction further resistance despite the regrouping of the greater part of his army at Ruthven between 17 and 20 April. Forced to disperse, the Jacobite soldiers went their separate ways, many of them shedding their weapons, uniforms and cause as they journeyed home to face the consequences of defeat. These were dire. For the next few months Cumberland and his subordinates had their men rape, murder and burn their way through the Highlands and Lowland areas believed sympathetic to Jacobitism. This may have been standard military practice for contemporary armies when dealing with rebels, yet it left a legacy of bitterness that was not quick to fade.

This dark aftermath was the beginning of a new trajectory for the British Isles. With the Jacobites beaten, Britain's government could turn all three nations' military energies outwards, and from the mid-1750s onwards

Scotland was harnessed to achieving Westminster's dreams of global empire. Scotland was, too, internally transformed by the events of 1745. The old ties between Highland chieftain and common clansman, and Lowland heritor and tenant farmer, which had been the basis of society for centuries, were in decline before the rising. After 1746 that decline became precipitous. Scotland was on track to becoming a class-based society.

Ireland, despite its apparent quiescence during the rebellion, was also far from untouched. Many expatriate Irishmen were involved in the French government's efforts hurriedly to put together an invasion of England. Others slipped through the royal navy's blockade and fought alongside the Scottish Jacobites at Culloden. When it was all over they were left with nowhere to go. As Charles Edward, haunted by bitterness and loss, drank himself to death in exile, the Jacobite cause withered and died with him. Where could Catholic Ireland now look for succour? Ultimately it turned to radical nationalism, something that would have been unthinkable before 1746. Like all the turning points in this series, 1745 irretrievably changed the scope of what was possible in the British Isles, and ultimately left no future generation untouched.

OTHER KEY DATES IN THIS PERIOD

1707 **Act of Union**. It may have been touted as an alliance of equals but, in reality, the creation of the kingdom of Great Britain saw a small Scottish representation grafted onto existing political structures at Westminster and Scottish interests subordinated to English politics. The constitutional fusion was also championed as being certain to deliver an immediate and substantial boost to Scotland's allegedly ailing economy (its problems may have been more apparent than real), which it singularly failed to do for nearly fifty years.

1713 **War of Succession**. The Peace of Utrecht brought the War of Spanish Succession (1702–13) to a close. This was a highly successful war for Britain in which France was defeated and forced to sue for peace. During the negotiations, however, French diplomats exploited British differences with their allies to extract relatively favourable terms. Britain nonetheless gained substantial imperial possessions and commercial concessions, though it alienated many of its wartime partners in the process.

1714 **Death of Anne**. Queen Anne, the last of the Protestant Stuarts in the main line of descent from James VI and I, died on 1 August and was succeeded by Georg Ludwig, elector of Hanover, the nearest (ostensible) Protestant by collateral descent. The transition from the Stuart to the Guelph dynasty was initially peaceful, and only marred by many Tories' coolness towards George I, whom they regarded with suspicion because of his religious indifference and the fact he was foreign.

1715 **Jacobite uprising**. Inspired by messianic visions of their own righteousness (not to mention consequent likelihood of success) and political hysteria, Jacobite forces rebelled in Scotland, subsequently provoking a rising in northern England. Though much larger in numbers than the 1745 uprising, the rebellion was poorly directed and relatively easily defeated by government forces. The Jacobite army disintegrated in February 1716 in a storm of mutual recrimination that hindered further Jacobite risings for the next thirty years.

1720 **Stocks crash.** Stimulated by excitement over the rise of French stocks and seduced by fanciful reports of great returns, investors poured huge amounts of money into the South Sea Company in Britain. The bursting of this bubble ruined a few speculators and caused serious losses to many more. As a result, British economic expansion was retarded for over a decade, and the Whig regime was nearly fatally compromised.

1736 **Scots lynch army captain.** Troops under the command of Captain John Porteous fired on an Edinburgh crowd protesting about the execution of a smuggler. Porteous was convicted of murder, but then reprieved by government order. Fearing he would be pardoned, a mob broke into the city gaol and lynched him, for which the city was heavily fined by Parliament. Anger in Scotland at this punishment resulted in a crisis in the Scottish Whig party and a surge in support for the Jacobites.

1739 **Mass starvation in Ireland.** The *bliain an áir* (great frost) struck Ireland in December, killing thousands and destroying stored winter food supplies. This was followed by a cold drought and the failure of the harvest in 1740, precipitating mass starvation. It is estimated that, by the time the crisis came to an end in 1741, a higher proportion of the population had died or fled overseas than as a result of the potato famine of the 1840s.

1776

America declares independence from the motherland

JEREMY BLACK

The American Declaration of Independence on 4 July 1776 was a key moment in the history not only of North America but also of Britain and the English-speaking world.

Until that moment, it had been possible that the fighting that had started outside Boston the previous year would end in a compromise, with George III backing down: the solution indeed sought by most of the American Patriots. However, the failure to reach compromise took the Patriots to revolution. What had seemed possibly a short-term conflict, ending when the British withdrew from Boston in March 1776, became instead a major civil war as the British Empire struck back with a concerted effort at regaining the lost colonies by force and as the Patriots opted for independence. In March 1776, Congress was still unwilling to accept a motion by George Wythe and Richard Henry Lee that King George III, not the ministry, nor Parliament, be seen as 'the author of our miseries'.

This became possible only because George III in effect disowned the Americans as rebels and treated them accordingly. British policies, including the ban on trade with the rebellious colonies, were designed to hurt, while the government's attempt to recruit subsidy forces (called foreign mercenaries in the Declaration of Independence) was associated directly with George, not least because these troops were Germans.

The rejection of British authority was symbolic as well as constitutional. On 9 July 1776, after the colonial assembly of New York gave its assent to the Declaration of Independence, the inhabitants of New York City pulled down a gilded equestrian statue of the king erected on Bowling Green in 1770 (its metal was to be used for cartridges), while, more generally, the royal arms were taken down, and usually treated with contempt. The king's name was removed from governmental and legal documents, royal portraits were reversed or destroyed, and there were mock trials, executions and funerals of the king, each a potent rejection of his authority.

In the short term, the impact of the Patriots' struggle for independence was serious in the extreme. It launched Britain into a war that it did not win, and that became strategically threatening when France (in 1778), Spain (in 1779), and the Dutch (in 1780) joined in as allies of the Americans. As a result, Britain, the great maritime power, was outnumbered at sea for the first time that century. The entire empire was under threat. The British lost positions in the West Indies, West Africa and the Mediterranean. Gibraltar faced a long siege. Britain's enemies also sought to strike at the heart of empire, with the French and Spaniards trying, unsuccessfully, to invade England in 1779. There was also the danger that resistance elsewhere to Britain, especially in India, would be encouraged by Britain's enemies. Indeed, the Americans struck at Canada in 1775, and the French at India in 1780.

Foreign challenge contributed directly to domestic crisis in Britain. A sense of state and society as tottering were captured by the Gordon Riots in 1780, which brought violent crowds to the centre of London, and by the collapse of the long-serving ministry of Lord North in 1782. This collapse led George III to threaten to abdicate and to go to Hanover, a threat that captured a sense of political and personal breakdown.

The long term, however, is the crucial perspective for 1776. American independence permanently transformed the nature of the British Empire. Prior to then, the bulk of the subjects of the British crown were of British, or at least European, descent, spoke English, were Christian, and were governed – albeit not to the satisfaction of many in North America – through local legislatures. American independence, however, revealed important deficiencies in the incorporating character of British Empire, deficiencies that shattered this empire and that were to be tested thereafter in relations with Ireland.

The loss of America was followed, as a result of repeated British successes in war between 1790 and 1815, particularly in India and at the expense of France and its allies, by the creation of a very different British Empire. In this, the bulk of the subjects were not of European descent, did not speak English, were not Christian, and were not governed through local legislatures. This very different imperialism had a major impact, not only on conquered areas, but also in Britain itself.

Furthermore, the American Declaration of Independence led to an important division in the British political tradition, one of great importance at the global level. The Declaration asserted a set of principles that suggested a radically different political system, one in which inherited privilege and power were replaced by a fairer society that was open to talent. In time, these values were to influence Britain powerfully, in part as a result of the American success. The example of liberty and freedom in North America was a potent one elsewhere, and not only for radicals like Tom Paine.

Moreover, the creation of an independent state in North America was to ensure the combination of dynamic expansion on the most promising open frontier of the western world with a political society that owed much to the eighteenth-century British Whig tradition. Whig freedoms, not least of self-government and self-expression, and a limitation on the power of the Church, were enshrined in the American constitution and, thereafter, remained key to American exceptionalism. Many people, of course, were excluded from the initial span of American liberty, most prominently slaves and Native Americans, but the prospectus of freedom proved one that was extendable to embrace the immigrant groups that entered North America in large numbers, many from the British Isles.

The hold of Whig freedoms on the American psyche has proved long-lived, so the events of 1776 helped ensure that British political culture remained crucial at the world scale in the early twenty-first century, even after Britain had been subsumed into an inflexible European superstate with individual freedoms shadowed by collectivist solutions.

Moreover, many of the liberal ideas that played a central role in British assumptions in the nineteenth century were taken up by American writers and policy makers from the 1940s, in part, initially, in criticism of the protectionism then shown by the British Empire. Drawing on Adam Smith and others, there was a focus on free trade, and the unfettered movement of money, as political and economic goods, and thus as central goals for government. There was also the notion of a benign and mutually beneficial world order: a goal that proved very difficult in practice, as is very much shown today in the Middle East, but that was an alternative to an empire simply of control, constraint and coercion.

The year 1776 also saw the publication of two very significant books. Adam Smith, a Glasgow professor, published *The Wealth of Nations*, which provided the basis for modern economic theory (an achievement marked by his appearance on the £20 note in 2007). Smith argued the case for the free trade that was to become the ideology of the nineteenth-century British state and economy. This was the cause of much prosperity, in Britain and around the world, as well as of some hardship on the part of those who suffered from the greater international trade and economic specialization that resulted.

Also published were the first volumes of the *Decline and Fall of the Roman Empire* by Edward Gibbon, an enlightened MP. In place of a cyclical theory of history, Gibbon's work suggested that progress was possible, and claimed that it was not inevitable that a fresh wave of barbarians would destroy Britain as had happened in Rome. He also argued that even if new barbarians brought down European civilization, it had already been reborn on the other side of the Atlantic.

OTHER KEY DATES IN THIS PERIOD

1756 **Start of the Seven Years War**. Britain suffered a national crisis as France was victorious in North America and the Mediterranean. Britain's humiliating failure to relieve a besieged garrison in Minorca led eventually to the court martial and execution of Admiral Byng. The government of the duke of Newcastle fell. William Pitt the Elder became the secretary of state.

1759 **Year of Victories**. The navy defeated French invasion fleets at Lagos and in Quiberon Bay, gaining naval mastery. British forces achieved several other major successes, including, crucially, James Wolfe's capture of Quebec. In Europe, British troops defeated the French at the battle of Minden and the 'bells of victory' rang out across Britain.

1763 **Peace of Paris**. This marked the end of the Seven Years War – with Britain victorious, winning major territorial gains from France and Spain, including New France (Canada) and Florida. Britain was now seen as the leading oceanic power and the anxieties of a few years earlier about the risks of French invasion were over.

1769 **Watt's patent for an improved steam engine**. James Watt's design was a major improvement on the earlier Newcomen steam engines. The first to perfect the separate condenser for the steam engine, Watt produced a machine that was more energy efficient and therefore less expensive to run. In the 1780s, he patented further innovations that gave a comparative uniformity of rotary motion, and thus increased the capacity of steam engines to drive industrial machinery.

1784 **William Pitt the Younger wins in a crucial general election**. Chosen as prime minister in 1783 by King George III, against the wishes of the Whig majority in the House of Commons, Pitt's success ended the political crisis. It ushered in a period of calmer parliamentary and ministerial politics that was to be reaffirmed by his electoral victories in 1790 and 1797. Pitt understood the need for sound finances.

His prudent fiscal management and a growth in overseas trade stabilized government finances.

1788-9 **Regency Crisis**. The recovery of George III ended the crisis caused by his attack of porphyria, which had been thought to betoken the onset of insanity. This prevented the creation of a regency and a Whig ministry. Pitt and his system were thus preserved, and stability was reaffirmed.

1793 **Britain and the French Revolutionary War**. Anxious about French moves in the Low Countries, Britain joined a coalition against France. This, however, was to be unsuccessful, and also increased domestic discontent. Meanwhile, the opening of the Monkland Canal stimulated the development of the Lanarkshire coalfield in order to serve the rapidly growing Glasgow market.

1832

The Reform Bill is passed

CATHERINE HALL

The late eighteenth century saw the loss of American colonies, new ideas about forms of government associated with the American Revolution and European Enlightenment, and economic and social changes associated with industrialisation, urbanisation and population growth.

It was a period of change on many fronts; the 1790s was a decade of both radicalism and reaction. New divisions of labour and the spread of industrial capitalism meant that discontent was widespread. Many artisans and labourers sought better working conditions and understood that parliamentary representation might be one way to secure them. Merchants, manufacturers and professional men, many of them Dissenters, faced with civil disabilities, wanted more say in political processes. First reactions to the revolution in France in 1789 were enthusiastic.

Tom Paine's *The Rights of Man* (1791–2), with its argument for universal manhood suffrage as the only legitimate basis for government, had been greeted with huge enthusiasm. Societies of working men had been established across England and Scotland seeking constitutional reform. But the execution of the French king and queen and the onset of the Terror shifted opinions dramatically, while war with France made criticism an unpatriotic action. Middle-class reformers retreated and the government embarked on a programme of repression, designed to crush radicalism at home.

It was only after the defeat of France in 1815 that popular radicalism re-emerged, led by figures such as the orator Henry Hunt and brilliant journalist and publicist William Cobbett, whose bitter critique of 'Old Corruption' – a metaphor for the systematic political oppression associated with heavy taxation, fiscal abuse, sinecures and monopolies – combined with his defence of 'Old England' made him one of the most powerful voices of the period. The Tory government, alarmed at the mobilization of the 'industrious classes' (artisans, cotton spinners, handloom weavers, small masters and tradesmen) cracked down again and the Peterloo massacre in 1819, when an unarmed crowd was fired upon, shocked middle-class reformers.

During the 1820s working men and women in the areas of the new factory system, whether in Yorkshire, Lancashire or Lanarkshire, struggled to come to terms with different forms of exploitation while in other urban centres such as London or Birmingham it was the decline of old patterns of skill and the spread of semi-skilled work done by women and children that disrupted established ways of living and working. As E.P. Thompson argued in his book *The Making of the English Working Class*, a sense of identity and shared consciousness gradually emerged, rooted in the experience of industrialization and urbanization, expressed through trade unions, the radical press, reading rooms and a culture of autodidacticism, all increasingly focused on the struggle for the vote for men. Women were expected to support the claims of their husbands, fathers and brothers.

Class, signifying new relations between masters and

men that operated in a market economy, was the key axis of politics in this period. Middle-class men had also been articulating their claims as propertied men, denizens of the new commercial and manufacturing order, to be represented in Parliament. James Mill sang his paean of praise in his influential *Essay on Government* (1819) to the rational and responsible middle-class men who would secure the right kind of polity for a modern world.

* * *

On 7 June 1832 King William IV reluctantly gave his assent to the Reform Act that extended the parliamentary franchise in England and Wales, marking the end of a period of high political tension across the country. Three years previously, in 1829, the Tory party had been split by the decision of Prime Minister Wellington and Home Secretary Robert Peel to grant Catholic Emancipation. Faced with the danger of civil war in Ireland, they chose to bow to popular pressure. The sanctity of 'the Protestant constitution' had been breached and Catholics could now sit at Westminster.

In July 1830 a revolution in France raised the spectre once again of disorder at home while violent disturbances among agricultural labourers in the south-east of England between August 1830 and December 1831 – the so-called Captain Swing riots when machines were smashed and burnt – terrified landed society. In Birmingham the banker Thomas Attwood had formed the Birmingham Political Union, an organization that mobilized middle- and working-class support, demanding parliamentary reform. The townspeople of places such as Birmingham, Manchester and Leeds sought representation, an end to corrupt patronage and a wider electorate, though there was little agreement as to who should be included.

Attwood wanted 'an army not less formidable than that

legally exhibited in Ireland, before which ministers were compelled to bend'. Wellington, however, a firm believer in aristocratic power and privilege, was convinced, despite much evidence to the contrary, that Britain 'possessed at the present moment a legislature which answered all the good purposes of legislation, and this to a greater degree than any legislature ever had answered in any country whatever', and that 'it possessed the full and entire confidence of the country.' His confidence was misplaced and the Whigs came into power knowing that some measure of reform was essential.

In March 1832 the Whig proposals for reform were presented to the House of Commons and were met with uproar: they were far more radical than had been expected. A £10 household franchise in the boroughs would secure the representation of many middle-class men while excluding working men. This was the kind of 'safe and practical reform' envisaged by the leading Whig reformer, Lord John Russell. It was clear to some of the more prescient radicals such as Henry Hetherington that the bill would not meet working-class demands.

His assessment was sharp. The Whigs, he argued, knew

that the old system could not last and desiring to estab-lish another as like it as possible, and also to keep their places, they framed a Bill, in the hope of drawing to the feudal aristocracy and the yeomen in the counties a large reinforcement of the middle class. The Bill was, in effect, an invitation to the shopocrats of the enfran-chised towns to join the Whigocrats of the country, and make common cause with them in keeping down the people, and thereby quell the rising spirit of democracy in England.

Other radicals, however, including key figures such as William Cobbett whose hugely influential *Political Register* played a vital part in popular politics, believed that the bill would make a difference and they must support it. It was the alliance from 'outside', of pressure from both middle- and working-class reformers across town and country, that ensured the success of reform. But Westminster still held the key and in the 1830s the House of Commons was at the political heart of Britain and its empire. A dramatic second reading in the Commons secured the bill by one vote as Thomas Babington Macaulay (later to be celebrated for his *History of England*) described to a friend,

> Such a scene as the division of last Tuesday I never saw, and never expect to see again. If I should live 50 years – the impression of it will be as fresh and sharp as if it had just taken place. It was like seeing Caesar stabbed in the Senate House, or seeing Oliver [Cromwell] taking the mace from the table, a sight to be seen only once and never forgotten.

Macaulay's speeches – arguing for 'reform in time', claiming that the particular genius of the constitution was its capacity to reform itself, and explaining why Britain, unlike its continental neighbours, had escaped revolution – were powerfully persuasive. 'All history is full of revolutions,' he argued,

> A portion of the community which had been of no account, expands and becomes strong. It demands a place in the system, suited, not to its former weakness, but to its present power. If this is granted, all is well. If this is refused, then comes the struggle between the young energy of one class, and the ancient privileges of another.

In the Commons there was sufficient support for reform, but the Lords with their Tory majority and strong contingent of bishops was a different matter. In September they threw out the bill and there were riots of workers in Derby, Nottingham and Bristol. As one Whig peer understood all too clearly, 'the bill at last must be carried by force or fear, not from conviction or affection.'

In May 1832 the prime minister, Earl Grey, faced with the intransigence of the Lords, made the shocking demand that the king should create fifty new peers as the only way to secure a majority. The king refused, Grey resigned and the duke of Wellington attempted unsuccessfully to form a government. These were the celebrated Days of May when Britain came very close to revolution. Petitions poured in from all parts of the country; the novel idea of a run on the banks – 'To stop the Duke go for Gold' was the slogan – was proposed, and the banker Nathan Mayer Rothschild had to come to the rescue; 200,000 delegates met in Birmingham and heard Attwood hint that armed insurrection might be necessary. The king had to return to Grey and the bill went through.

Why did it matter? The Reform Bill, as John Bright the Quaker reformer put it, was 'not a good bill, though a great bill when it passed', for its implications were substantial. The same people went on ruling Britain, the aristocracy maintained their dominance in government until the 1870s, patronage did not disappear and nor did deference. Few middle-class men went into the Commons. Yet something very important had happened. An aristocratic Whig government had to bow to popular pressure, just as the Tories had done in 1829. They had opened a door that they would have much preferred to keep closed. They hoped the business was finished; of course it was not.

Many of those working-class reformers who had been bitterly disillusioned by the betrayal of their hopes with the 1832 Act were pivotal to the formation of the Chartist movement that sought universal male suffrage and played a vital part in the politics of the later 1830s and 1840s. The Reform Act specified for the first time that it was men who could vote. In August 1832 a petition to the House of Commons from Mary Smith of Stanmore asked for the vote for 'every unmarried woman having that pecuniary qualification whereby the other sex is entitled to the said franchise'. Smith was a wealthy Yorkshire lady and saw no reason why those who paid taxes should not have a share in the election of their representatives. She had no success but her petition was symptomatic of new claims being made by women, claims that would not be met for more than a century.

Meanwhile the newly enfranchised middle class did flex their muscles on the slavery question. In the election that followed the Reform Act supporters of anti-slavery organized on a large scale to ensure that candidates would pledge to vote for emancipation. In the new session of Parliament slavery was abolished, though apprenticeship, a system of forced labour, remained.

Meanwhile, decisions about the character of the nation had repercussions far beyond. In 1833 in debates over the new Charter Act for India it was made clear that while representative government was appropriate for white Britons, a benevolent despotism was the most suitable form of government for India, while in Ireland, that 'metropolitan colony', new forms of coercion were introduced that would not have been tolerated on the mainland. The year 1832 stands for a critical moment in the history of both nation and empire.

OTHER KEY DATES IN THIS PERIOD

1800 **Act of Union**. This was forced through the Irish parliament by British Prime Minister Pitt after the failure of the United Irishmen's rebellion of 1798. The Irish were now represented at Westminster. Pitt promised Catholic emancipation would follow but the entrenchment of the Protestant ascendancy meant that this was long withheld.

1807 **Abolition of slave trade on British ships**. 1807 finally saw the abolition of the British slave trade after campaigns on an unprecedented scale had been waged on and off from 1787, led by Clarkson and Wilberforce. 'The sense of the nation has pressed abolition upon our rulers,' was the judgement of the influential *Edinburgh Review*. The declaration of the Republic of Haiti also played a part, for French competition in the Caribbean sugar trade was much reduced.

1815 **Battle of Waterloo**. This was the final defeat of Napoleon at Waterloo and the triumph of Britain as a world power. Conquests in the Caribbean, India and the Cape meant that the empire had expanded greatly and Britain ruled approximately a quarter of the world's population.

1819 **Peterloo Massacre**. The end of the French wars saw extensive demobilization and unemployment. Political demands first articulated by radicals in the 1790s were revived and a mass meeting in St Peter's Fields in Manchester, addressed by the great orator Henry Hunt and demanding political reform, turned into the massacre of Peterloo when the militia fired on unarmed protestors.

1829 **Catholic Emancipation**. This was finally granted after years of agitation in Ireland, led by Daniel O'Connell. 'We are men and deserve to be free' was the cry of the Catholic Association, which mobilized huge numbers of men with the support of 'their' women across Ireland and forced the civil equality of Catholics on an unwilling Tory administration. A struggle for repeal of the Union soon began, however, for emancipation did not put an end to Ireland's grievances.

1833 **An end to slavery.** A rebellion of the enslaved in Jamaica in 1831 and a popular campaign across Britain led to the abolition of slavery from 1 August 1834. Forced apprenticeship (brought to an end in 1838) and £20 million in compensation convinced the West Indian interest to accept this. A Charter Act for India increased the role of the British government in India and reduced the power of the East India Company.

1846 **Repeal of Corn Laws.** Another popular campaign, this time spearheaded by middle-class free traders, resulted in the repeal of the Corn Laws, long regarded as a symbol of the continuing power of the landowning classes. Prime Minister Peel's decision split the Tory party, opening the way for Disraeli's rise to power.

1848 **Revolution in Europe.** Revolutions erupted across continental Europe and there were extensive fears in Britain that Chartist demands for parliamentary reform, including a universal male franchise, could not be contained. On 10 April London was barricaded with troops at the ready but in the event the demonstration on Kennington Common presented no threat.

1849 **Advancement for women.** Bedford College was opened, initially to train women teachers, and among its pupils in the years to come were Barbara Leigh Smith and George Eliot. This was one of the signs of the development of the women's movement that emerged in the 1850s, committed to education, employment and suffrage for women alongside an end to the sexual double standard.

1851

The Great Exhibition transforms Britain

PETER MANDLER

Traditionally, the Crystal Palace has been seen as the starting point of a great Victorian era of peace, industry and empire – and so it was, though we now know that it was also something much more. This spectacular centrepiece of the Great Exhibition of the Works of Industry of All Nations, opened by Queen Victoria on 1 May 1851 and straddling the year until it closed its doors officially on 11 October, celebrated with more than a touch of complacency the peaceful triumph of Britain's unique compound elite, part-aristocratic, part-capitalist. Britain had escaped the revolutions that had plunged continental Europe into social division and civil war in 1848, and the planning and execution of the Great Exhibition in 1851 was naturally timed to remind the world of that fact.

The festival celebrated Britain's industrial supremacy, both in its form and its content. A vast shed – a blend of greenhouse, railway terminus and museum, half again as long as the Millennium Dome built 150 years later – the Crystal Palace was constructed from prefabricated and interchangeable parts made of the most modern materials, iron and glass. It was deliberately filled with products of great size and ingenuity to shock and awe – huge blocks of coal, the largest steam locomotives, hydraulic presses and steam-hammers, a scale model of the Liverpool docks with 1,600 miniature ships in full rigging; sewing machines, ice-making machines, cigarette-rolling machines, machines to mint medals and machines to fold envelopes.

If the exhibition was open to all nations, the results were confidently expected to demonstrate British superiority. The aim was to show the global dominance that Britain had achieved not by rapine or conquest but by virtue and hard work – steam engines and cotton-spinning machines were held up by the novelist Thackeray as 'trophies of her bloodless wars'.

But that complacent picture does not capture the sheer exuberant messiness of the Crystal Palace, or the full range of excitements through which it prefigures the modern life that we live today. Though responsibility for the Great Exhibition was vested in a Royal Commission crammed with the great and the good, and led by the prince consort, a free press kept up a loud and rowdy running commentary, and every segment of a diverse and disputatious public opinion – including the large majority who were formally excluded from political representation – offered up its own views. When after three weeks of more exclusive viewing by the 'respectable' public the Crystal Palace was opened to 'shilling tickets' on 26 May, the floodgates were opened and six million people poured through them in the next four months.

In fact, the Great Exhibition gave a decisive push to physical mobility – travel to it has been called 'the largest movement of population ever to have taken place in Britain' – and it can be said to have kick-started the entire

apparatus of the modern tourist industry: the railway journey, the package holiday, the hotel (or at least the B&B)
and the restaurant were all to be transformed from elite
into popular experiences. Thomas Cook alone brought
165,000 people to the Crystal Palace from the Midlands
on cheap excursion trains.

To orient these strangers, street signs of the modern type
had to be invented. To comfort them, public lavatories
were for the first time installed. London, which had been
used to dominating national attention in the eighteenth
century but had had to share the spotlight with the great
cities of the north in the early nineteenth, once again
became the nation's cynosure. In the following years, it
increased its share of the national population and began
to resume a stature that it has never since lost.

What had the masses come to see, and what did they
make of it? Undoubtedly they were awed by the great
machines and demonstrations of power. They would also
have been aware of the formidable police presence – anything from 200 to 600 policemen. On the other hand,
they had a huge variety of sights to choose from – there
were 100,000 exhibits – and could gravitate freely to those
that pleased or intrigued them. These were often trinkets
and gadgets on a human scale that people could relate to,
could imagine in their homes: consumer goods of paper
and glass, new styles of furniture, brands of toothpaste
and soap.

A visit to the Crystal Palace was not supposed to be a
shopping expedition. Exhibitors were not allowed to
display prices or to sell over the counter. But supply and
demand could not be so easily kept apart. Brochures,
posters, trade cards and price sheets proliferated. Outside the Crystal Palace, the rest of London did its best
to capitalize on the visitors. Historians now think that
the modern age of advertising was opened by the Great

Exhibition – the primitive shop signs, handbills and small-print newspaper adverts of the eighteenth century were gradually transformed by a panoply of new technologies, leading to the billboard, the illustrated display advertisement, the department-store window. Among the visitors in 1851 was a 20-year-old draper's apprentice from Yorkshire, William Whiteley, who was inspired to move his theatre of operations to London and who in the 1860s expanded his draper's shop in Westbourne Grove into Britain's first department store, Whiteley's, the Universal Provider.

These surging crowds and their clamour for goods and thrills drew snooty criticisms of vulgarity, and we have long been familiar with comments such as John Ruskin's – he called the palace 'a cucumber-frame between two chimneys' – and William Morris' – he called it 'wonderfully ugly'. The likes of Ruskin and Morris were offended because the palace's projectors had portrayed it as a chance to refine popular tastes, whereas they saw only crowd-pleasing cheapness.

Thanks to the railway, visiting the Crystal Palace was not only a national but an international phenomenon. Rail connections between Paris and London had been completed just prior to 1851 and in the year of the exhibition the numbers of travellers between France and England nearly doubled to 260,000. The international nature of the exhibits gave visitors a powerful sense of a newly wide world – and, with steam facilitating travel both by land and by sea, a shrinking world.

The British Empire was literally at the centre of the Crystal Palace, with an Indian Court filled with fine materials and finished goods meant explicitly to strengthen trade between metropole and empire. These were hardly trophies of bloodless wars. But there was a strong streak of idealism present, an idealism that did see free trade between equals as the civilized substitute for war. Exhibits from America drew special attention to an emerging power, now seen less as rebellious offspring, more as a potential trading partner. Sensationally, the Americans' McCormick reaping machine beat its British rivals in a competition, harvesting twenty acres of corn in a day.

Visitors of 1851 got a glimpse of what we call globalization. The telegraph was on display – used to communicate from one end of the giant structure to the other – and contemporaries were well aware of its potential use for global communications, talking of a forthcoming 'network of wires' and a 'never-ceasing interchange of news'. In about twenty years, that network would span continents; in about fifty it would span the world.

We are now also better aware that the Crystal Palace had an afterlife, reconstructed on a new site in south London – and serving for another eighty years as the 'Palace of the People', responsible among other things for inaugurating the dinosaur craze (the life-size models are among the few fragments of the Victorian period to survive on the site) and for pioneering a dizzying range of commercial entertainments, from high-wire acts to aeronautical displays. Even if we confine ourselves to the year 1851, the Crystal Palace can be seen as a pivot on which swings a door that opens on to the modernity we enjoy today.

What we can see more clearly now than people could then was that the generally optimistic hopes of projectors and visitors, while realized to an extraordinary extent, also cast darker shadows – the 100,000 exhibits have multiplied a hundred thousand-fold in our consumer society, for ill as well as for good; the number of police have multiplied too; internationalism and the shrinking globe did not betoken world peace; and just imagine the carbon footprint left by all those machines . . .

* * *

The country in which the Crystal Palace was built in 1851 was the United Kingdom of Great Britain and Ireland – as it had been since 1801, when the Union with Ireland was inaugurated, and would be until the partition of Ireland after the First World War. The great social and economic changes of the Industrial Revolution had bonded Wales, Scotland and England more firmly together; South Wales, Lowland Scotland and the north of England, in particular, had all become more urban and industrial in character, more liberal in politics, and more nonconformist in religion.

Nationalism was not a potent force in any of these areas. But Ireland had been an exception in all these respects earlier in the century, and by 1851 had become even more so. Hit by the holocaust of the Irish famine in the late 1840s, Ireland's population would dwindle over the rest of the century as emigrants poured out of the country. Between 1841 and 1901 Britain's population grew from 26.7 million to 41.5 million; Ireland's dropped from 8.2 million to 4.5 million.

While living standards were rising in the second half of the nineteenth century for most of the population, these rises were distributed unequally – probably more unequally than at any other point in British history. The top 0.5 per cent of the population accounted for 25 per cent of the nation's income. In comparison, the same share is earned by the top 10 per cent today. Wealth was distributed still more unequally. There was a class of super-rich, known as the 'upper ten thousand', comprised mainly of landowners and bankers. Three-quarters of the population would have been employed in manual working-class occupations, most of the rest as shopkeepers and clerks.

Opportunities for social mobility were severely limited, and living conditions for most remained cramped and unhealthy. As a result, it was not only the Irish who emigrated – emigration from all parts of the British Isles escalated steeply over this half-century, especially to the United States, Canada and Australia.

However, Britain was very far from a nation in decline in this period. Its share of world manufacturing output held up remarkably well, at just under a fifth of the total in 1900, practically where it had been in 1860. The advent of universal, free and compulsory education in the 1870s and 1880s meant that literacy became nearly total by the end of the century.

Despite extensions of the franchise in 1867 and 1884, however, not even all adult males were entitled to vote, and some adult males had more votes than others. The United Kingdom in this period was in many respects 'free' but still unequal.

OTHER KEY DATES IN THIS PERIOD

1854 **The Crimean War begins**. Despite the high hopes expressed at the Crystal Palace, the second half of the century was not a period of unbroken peace. The Crimean War pitted Britain and France against Russian expansion into the Ottoman Empire. It lasted two years, left contemporaries with a big bill and an inquest into military disorganization, and bequeathed to posterity Florence Nightingale, the Charge of the Light Brigade (at the battle of Balaclava) and, indeed, the balaclava (the headwarmers knitted for British troops to guard against cold Russian nights).

1857 **Indian Mutiny**. Only a mutiny, of course, from the British point of view – now more frequently called a 'rebellion'. Sepoys – locally recruited soldiers – protested against conditions in the East India Company's army. A direct result was the end of East India Company rule and the incorporation of India into the formal empire.

1867 **Second Reform Act**. Although this Act gave the vote to only about a third of adult males in England and Wales, it marked the point at which the United Kingdom began to think of itself as a democracy. But it also underscored the inequitable treatment of Ireland, where fewer than a sixth of adult males got the vote in a separate Act.

1869 **Origins of women's suffrage**. Often overlooked in the shadow of the Second Reform Act, a reform of the municipal franchise in 1869 gave the vote in local elections to unmarried women who were heads of households. This betokened a growing role for women in social and political affairs below the parliamentary level.

1884 **Third Reform Act**. A further extension of the franchise to adult males, it was followed by a Redistribution Act that created equal electoral districts, more or less the electoral system as we know it today.

1889 **London Dock Strike**. Although the Trades Union Congress can be dated back to 1868, the London Dock Strike brought trade unionism into the centre of public life for the first time, largely because it demonstrated that 'ordinary' workers could strike as well – not only skilled workers seeking to protect their trade privileges.

1896 **Origins of the tabloid press**. The Harmsworth brothers (later lords Northcliffe and Rothermere) founded the *Daily Mail*, the first of a new breed of cheap and cheerful newspapers. It cost a halfpenny – half the cost of the standard cheap newspaper – and specialized in shorter human-interest stories and a vigorously populist editorial tone.

1899 **The Boer War breaks out**. The decades of 'peace' since the Crimean War had been marred by repeated colonial wars; however, these had required little British manpower. This colonial war – against Dutch settlers in southern Africa– required a serious mobilization and, like the Crimean War, it left behind a bitter taste in human and financial costs, as well as concerns about Britain's war-fighting capacity.

1916

The Somme, and Lloyd George founds his coalition

GERARD DEGROOT

The British, it is often said, went to war with Rupert Brooke and came home with Siegfried Sassoon. While the aphorism seems to encapsulate the evolution of national consciousness from the naive patriotism of 1914 to the bitterness of 1918, it is too simplistic to explain the change that came over Britain as a result of the First World War. That change manifested itself most profoundly in 1916 – a pivotal year that neatly divides old Britain from the modern nation of today.

Poets are seldom accurate barometers of national temper. The average British soldier did not romanticize, like Brooke, the idea of dying in some foreign field that would be forever England. The millions who volunteered in the first two years of the war did so for various reasons, many of them more mundane then we might think. Patriotism was undoubtedly a big factor, with most displaying a dispassionate willingness to serve their country in its hour of need. Others volunteered for less sublime reasons like pressure from employers or girlfriends, the lure of masculine adventure or simply the need for a job.

Most soldiers did not mirror Brooke's romanticism, so they didn't suffer Sassoon's bitterness. That feeling arose because of the deep chasm between expectation and experience – what Sassoon's friend Wilfred Owen called 'the old lie'. The war poets discovered that it was not 'sweet' to die for one's country and their poems reflect the sense of betrayal that came with that discovery. The common soldier, in contrast, discovered something different, namely that service implied citizenship. War experience was for them an entry in the balance sheet of life, to be compensated by peacetime recognition.

The millions who volunteered in the first year of the war were ready for battle in 1916. They were the soldiers of the Somme who walked into German machine-gun fire on 1 July. On that day, the British army experienced the worst losses in its history – 57,000 casualties, of whom 19,000 were dead. The scale of death inspired a long, bitter post-mortem.

For the past ninety years, the British have argued over alternatives and desperately sought scapegoats. In truth, however, long casualty lists were the inevitable result of the conjunction of industrialized war with democratized service. By 1916, Europe had millions willing to fight and the industrial capacity to kill them. War became a machine of death for which human beings were the fuel.

The scale of death forced Britain to become a nation at war. The millions who took up arms had left factories, fields, docks and offices. Their place was taken by the old, the young, the infirm and, notably, by women. Much has been made of the influx of women in the workplace, and the emancipation that supposedly led from it. In truth, however, the idea of women working was nothing new, though never before had British women performed work so important. Its importance lies not so much in the effect it had upon the women themselves, but rather in the implications it had for the nation as a whole. In ways seldom recognized, Britain was rescued by her women.

By 1916, it was clear that victory would be achieved not on the battlefield but in the factories and farms. Success would go to the nation best able to mobilize its population for the single purpose of sustaining the war effort. The army congregated in France and Belgium was Britain's largest city, bar London. Like any city, it needed food, clothing, transport, a legal system and medical and pastoral care. Unlike any other city, it consumed a prodigious supply of munitions and produced nothing except death. All of its needs had to be provided by those back at home, from a workforce diminishing in numbers and skill.

Mobilization demanded organization and a heretofore unthinkable degree of government intervention. Britain began the war under the misguided assumption that it would be short and profitable, and that those at home would not feel its pain. Indeed, the phrase 'home front' was seldom used before 1914. It was invented to describe a peculiar implication of industrialized war that became blindingly evident in 1916. 'Business as usual' gave way to a comprehensive system of government control. Regulations affected nearly every aspect of life, including where a person lived and worked, what he or she earned and bought, the food they ate and the beer they drank.

These controls spelled the death of liberalism. That philosophy was based on the sanctity of individual freedom, yet it was clear that the rights of the individual could not withstand the demands of war. The most important symbol of sacrifice came in January 1916 with the passage of the Military Service Act, which imposed conscription on all men aged between 18 and 41. The right to choose whether to fight for one's country, arguably the most sacred individual freedom, was cast aside with surprisingly little dissent. Conscription, it should be noted, was not just a way to supply soldiers for the army; it was also a way to control the workforce at home.

The assault upon liberalism had dire consequences for the Liberal Party. The party's demise was apparent virtually from the start of the war, but was dramatically confirmed by the formation, on 6 December 1916, of a new coalition led by David Lloyd George. The previous coalition, formed by Herbert Asquith in 1915, had brought the Tories and (significantly) Labour into the government, but was essentially a desperate attempt to preserve liberalism by other means.

Asquith had sought to improvise his way to victory, intervening in the economy only when disaster threatened. The futility of that was revealed by the Somme offensive, which lasted for three months and resulted in 400,000 British casualties, in the process putting huge pressure on the British economy. Lloyd George used the issue of war management to shove Asquith aside. The party was cleaved by the coup, the purists following Asquith, the realists Lloyd George.

A new prime minister meant a new, more presidential, style. Asquith had desperately tried to preserve the ideal of cabinet government, even though it was ill suited to wartime centralization. Lloyd George, despite his liberal sympathies, was authoritarian – the type of leader ideal for the conduct of war. He brought to Downing Street the same dynamism, creativity and determination that he had earlier exhibited at the Ministry of Munitions and the War Office. This implied a willingness to slaughter sacred cows – nothing was allowed to stand in the way of victory.

Centralization brought homogenization. Britain became a single nation driven by a single purpose. While much local pride was invested in, for instance, the Royal Welch Fusiliers and the Scots Guards, in truth regional differences were smothered by wartime unity and the democracy of death. War fostered a genuine sense of Britishness. The one notable exception was, of course, Ireland, where nationalists turned wartime calamity into opportunity. The Easter Rising of 1916 never had a hope of achieving its immediate aim of separation, but did change the face of Irish politics forever.

The sacrifice of youth first manifested on the Somme in 1916 continues to haunt Britain. That loss has, over the years, obscured a death at least as profound, namely the demise of the liberal ethos. Liberalism would survive the war but would no longer be the guiding principle of government. Wartime intervention carried the undeniable accolade of success – mobilization had won the war. In time, the lessons of war would be applied to the problems of peace, with the accompanying expectation that every calamity affecting society demanded governmental response. The welfare of the collective would be promoted at the cost of individual freedom.

One of the most striking lessons of 1916 was the ability of the nation to withstand massive loss. Ubiquitous death did not, as in Russia, inspire revolution, but rather brought out a stoic determination to persevere. The soldiers who survived wanted afterwards to join the system, not to destroy it. For them, wartime service came to imply the right to a political voice, increasingly expressed through the Labour Party. 'Remember the Trenches', a Labour poster enjoined in 1923. In a similar but less pronounced way, the women who once filled shells in the munitions factories were not radicalized by their experience, but they did gain a sense of service that was a step on the road to full citizenship.

'I think of you the same and always shall,' wrote Marian

Allen in homage to her lover who died in the First World War. That sentiment seems appropriate not just to her loss, but also to the entire generation that died in 1916. The soldiers in khaki are frozen in time, forever young, forever innocent. The Britain they once inhabited, however, travelled resolutely forwards, on rails laid in 1916. The nation they had volunteered to protect was never restored. Today, the world of Asquith seems quaint, that of Lloyd George utterly familiar.

* * *

The half-century from 1900 to 1949 brought the First and Second World Wars and the Depression. Those three calamities left Britain devastated. In 1900, it was a great power, in control of a massive empire and the largest navy in the world. By 1949, it was a second-rate power, helpless to stop the inevitable tide of decolonization. Once the world's banker, Britain had become a major borrower, dependent upon foreign loans to keep the economy afloat.

These great developments are undoubtedly important to an understanding of Britain during the period, but perhaps not as important as the motor car, the washing machine, the vacuum cleaner and the cinema. Real life is shaped by trivialities. Great events fill newspapers and history books precisely because they are extraordinary and, as such, a far cry from the mundane lives that most people lead. The rituals of everyday life hold society together and provide stability in a threatening world. Despite the wars, depression and political upheaval of the period 1900–49, most British people got on with life and even prospered.

Much can be learned from studying changes in the British diet. During the First World War, the bread ration was *limited* to seven pounds per man per week. Bread, eaten with a bit of dripping, was the staple food for the working class. Meat was a rare treat, and vegetables even rarer. Oranges were given at Christmas precisely because they were so uncommon. No wonder that only 34 per cent of the British male population was technically fit for front-line service in 1914.

War, ironically, was good for the health of the British population. The shock of the Boer War, when Britain struggled to gather together an army healthy enough to fight, inspired the Liberal welfare reforms of 1908–14. Similar concern was shown after the First World War, though the scale of reform was limited by financial crisis. The Second World War inspired the creation of the welfare state, with its aim of care from cradle to grave.

At the same time that health improved, so too did quality of life. The washing machine and the vacuum cleaner relieved some of the drudgery of housework, while improving hygiene in the home. By 1939, there were more than one million cars on the road. That, combined with improvements in rail services, made travel around the country much more common. So, too, did the increased provision of paid holidays. Meanwhile, cinemas and dance halls provided escapist excitement for those otherwise trapped in monotony. In the interwar period, one-third of the British population went to the cinema at least once a week.

By 1949, it was difficult to define what was 'great' about Britain. A half-century of war and depression rendered the country weak and destitute. The average citizen, however, was better educated, healthier, and lived an altogether richer life mid-century than his or her ancestors in 1900. The decline of a nation did not, in other words, mean the decline of a people.

OTHER KEY DATES IN THIS PERIOD

1901 **Death of Queen Victoria.** This provided a symbolic end to an era. Meanwhile, the continued difficulties the British army was experiencing in taming Boer forces in South Africa raised serious doubts about the defence of the British Empire. After the war, Britain forged alliances of a sort with France, Russia and Japan in order to protect its colonies in Asia and Africa. Meanwhile, the poor quality of army recruits focused attention on the need for social welfare reforms, or what became known as 'national efficiency'.

1908 **Campbell-Bannerman's resignation.** The Liberal prime minister's departure brought Herbert Asquith to Downing Street and David Lloyd George to the exchequer. The change ushered in the phase of 'New Liberalism' inspired by Lloyd George and Winston Churchill. The government embarked upon the most radical programme of reform since 1870, eventually introducing legislation covering employment, housing, pensions and health – all financed by a revolutionary 'People's Budget'.

1924 **First Labour administration.** After an election in December 1923 resulted in a hung parliament, the first ever Labour government took office in January, with Ramsay MacDonald as its leader. His government was too weak to achieve anything of substance, but did demonstrate, by its very existence, that Labour had supplanted the Liberals as the party of the left. A second election in October returned the Tories to power and further crippled the Liberal Party.

1929 **World depression.** A general election in May resulted in Labour winning the most seats, though not a clear majority. MacDonald returned to Downing Street. The new government's plans for social reform were rendered moot by the Wall Street Crash in October, which ushered in worldwide economic depression. Unemployment steadily rose, reaching 2.5 million by the following year.

1931 **Formation of the National Government.** The worsening economic crisis and steadily rising unemployment figures placed enormous pressure upon the Labour government. With Britain on the verge of bankruptcy, the May Committee advised cuts in unemployment benefits. In August, the government broke up over the question of these cuts. A national government was formed that was essentially conservative, though MacDonald remained prime minister.

1940 **Chamberlain's resignation.** A succession of military defeats, combined with accumulated disillusionment over the failure of appeasement, resulted in the resignation of Neville Chamberlain as prime minister. Winston Churchill formed a coalition government notable for Labour's enthusiastic support. Labour was rewarded with a number of important domestic ministries, in particular the appointment of Ernest Bevin as minister of labour. British cities were bombarded by the Luftwaffe.

1942 **Beveridge Report.** The stunning defeat of the German Wehrmacht at El Alamein by British forces in November 1942 was followed by the publication of *Social Insurance and Allied Services*, commonly known as the Beveridge Report. It laid the foundation for the welfare state and was hugely popular among all classes in wartime Britain.

1945 **Labour landslide.** The end of war in Europe was immediately followed by a general election that resulted in the shock defeat of Churchill's Conservative Party. The landslide victory of the Labour Party further solidified support for the programme of reform that was recommended in the Beveridge Report. The election, which was surprising at the time, now seems the understandable expression of the collectivist sympathies encouraged during the war.

1946 **Creation of the National Health Service.** At the peak of its popularity, the Labour government under Clement Attlee pushed through a series of social welfare reforms, including, most notably, the National Health Service Act. On another front, the government embarked upon a comprehensive programme of nationalization of key industries, including steel and coal. To fund the reforms, the government imposed severe austerity measures.

1956

Suez signals the dying days of empire

PAT THANE

We can't isolate British history in the second half of the twentieth century from world events. The year 1956 began with signs that the Cold War was thawing. In January, Nikita Khrushchev, first secretary of the Communist Party of the USSR, admitted and denounced Stalin's crimes. In April Khrushchev and the Soviet premier, Bulganin, made the first visit to Britain of Soviet leaders since 1917. They aroused popular curiosity and the concern of the security services who, apparently unknown to the prime minister, Anthony Eden, sent a frogman, Lionel 'Buster' Crabb, to inspect their ship. He did not return and his headless body was later found floating along the coast near Portsmouth. Doubts over how much Soviet attitudes really had softened were justified in October, when the Hungarian uprising against Russian domination was brutally suppressed.

The disastrous attempted invasion of Suez signified that Britain was no longer a first-rank power. In July President Nasser of Egypt nationalized the company that owned the Suez Canal, which was jointly owned by the British and

French governments. Nasser was desperate to avenge the US and Britain's refusal to offer Egypt financial support following its decision to sign an arms deal with the USSR; seizing control of the most direct route to Britain's colonies in the East appeared to be the best way of going about it. Tension was also fanned by British concerns over Egyptian support for insurgents in Aden and Nasser's support of the Algerians' bloody battle for independence from France.

What followed was a shattering blow to British prestige. Following international attempts at mediation, in October, Israel, who feared Nasser's growing strength, attacked Egypt in secret collusion with France and Britain. When Nasser refused to back down, British and French forces bombed and invaded Egypt. There was an international outcry, strong opposition in all political parties in Britain and France, condemnation from the United Nations (UN) and, most strongly, from the US. The value of sterling collapsed, the invaders were forced to withdraw ignominiously and Eden resigned, being replaced by Harold Macmillan.

Britain was fighting several other conflicts in its dwindling colonies. In Malaya a communist-led insurgency began in 1948 and ended with independence in 1957. In Cyprus, Greek nationalist violence led to their spiritual leader Archbishop Makarios' deportation to the Seychelles in March 1956. After Suez, Macmillan began to negotiate independence for Cyprus, achieved in 1960. Kenyan nationalism led to Mau Mau guerrilla terrorism between 1952 and 1957. The British army failed to quell the uprising and Kenya gained independence in 1960. In September 1956, Britain agreed to independence for the Gold Coast, now Ghana. A 'wind of change' was indeed blowing through Africa, as Macmillan put it in 1960 – though not in South Africa where he coined the phrase. In 1956, Reverend Trevor Huddleston left the country, following the publication of his bestselling exposé of hardening apartheid, *Naught for Your Country*. For the next thirty-five years he was a leader of the British anti-apartheid movement. Meanwhile six European countries moved towards signing the Treaties of Rome (March 1957). Yet Britain held aloof, giving priority to its ties with the Commonwealth and the US.

The mid-1950s saw important transformations within Britain, with unprecedented improvements in living standards and consumption. More houses were built, though in 1961 3.2 million people in England and Wales still did not have a fixed bath or shower. More people took holidays, some of them abroad. More owned vacuum cleaners, washing machines and television sets. Commercial television had been introduced in 1955, so there was now a choice of two channels. Recognizing that more people could save, the 1956 budget introduced Premium Bonds, described by the future Labour leader, Harold Wilson, as a 'squalid raffle'. Leisure patterns changed: attendance at cinemas, spectator sports and religious services fell, while 'do-it-yourself' and gardening grew. Recorded crime also grew, but so did the efficiency of detection and recording.

Full employment and prosperity encouraged immigration from poorer Commonwealth countries. But immigrants from the Caribbean, India and Pakistan often faced hostility; serious racial violence in Notting Hill and Nottingham led to legislation to restrict immigration in 1958.

In general, prosperity bred contentedness – as Harold Macmillan put it in 1957: 'Let us be frank about it, most of our people have never had it so good' – but also the confidence to criticize. Easter 1956 saw the first protest against Britain's nuclear weapons programme, leading to the foundation of the Campaign for Nuclear Disarmament in 1958. The nuclear issue exacerbated splits in the Labour

Party, which was going through a bout of internecine struggle that rendered it unelectable in the 1950s.

The Conservative governments of the 1950s, sometimes reluctantly, sustained the welfare state. They feared that its most popular feature, the National Health Service, was wastefully expensive. However, the Guillebaud Committee, established to examine this proposition, reported in 1956 that there was no 'widespread extravagance' in the NHS and no need for change. The Conservatives did most for health with the 1956 Clean Air Act, which reduced air pollution – a major cause of death, notably during the great London 'smog' of 1952. They also achieved a massive increase in local authority house building. Clement Attlee's governments had built relatively little, mainly due to their determination to build to high standards; the council houses built in the 1950s were of poorer quality, creating the 'sink estates' that Conservatives later condemned.

The inadequacies of the post-war welfare state were becoming obvious, even to some of its strongest sympathizers. Richard Titmuss, Labour Party welfare policy adviser, demonstrated that the middle classes gained most from the welfare state and that much poverty remained. In 1957, J.E. Floud, A.H. Halsey and F.M. Martin published *Social Class and Educational Opportunity*, establishing that the 1944 Education Act had not greatly improved the educational opportunities of the working class. The main beneficiaries of the 11-plus examination and grammar school education were middle-class boys, while girls of all classes fared worst. There were fewer grammar school places for them, so they had to score better than boys in the 11-plus. The great majority of children who left the lower-status secondary modern schools at 15 had few or no formal qualifications. The numbers in higher education were far fewer than in other high-income countries.

These findings led to the introduction of comprehensive education by a Labour government in the mid-1960s.

Nevertheless, work and relative prosperity gave working-class youth greater independence. Youth culture was reinvented, breeding moral panics about 'juvenile delinquency', stimulated by shock at the 'teddy-boy' style of young men with long hair, sideburns, Edwardian-style draped jackets and narrow trousers. The film *Blackboard Jungle* did little to quell the fears of Middle England. Released in Britain in 1956, it portrayed violence in US high schools, accompanied by a soundtrack by the first major rock 'n' roll phenomenon, Bill Haley and his Comets. In 1957 Haley and his Comets toured Britain to a frenzied reception.

Despite these concerns over the moral fibre of young men, most spent two years in National Service, sometimes dying in the post-colonial wars. The rest spent much of their time in work or education and married in larger numbers than ever. There were low levels of 'illegitimacy' in an atmosphere of strong social disapproval of sex before marriage.

Older, more celebrated and more disaffected were the 'angry young men' of the arts. Colin Wilson's *The Outsider*, published in 1956, was an anguished, if often obscure, assault on contemporary society. It appeared in the same week as the first performance of John Osborne's play *Look Back in Anger*, a more overt assault on accepted conventions. Noel Coward's wholly conventional *Nude with Violin*, first performed shortly after, attracted bigger, if less intellectual, audiences.

Angry young women were fewer, or anyway less visible and celebrated. Women's campaigning for equality was weaker than in the 1920s and 1930s, but it had not disappeared. In 1955 women in the civil service, local government and teaching gained equal pay, for which they had campaigned for decades. Hopes that the private sector would follow were not fulfilled. In *Women's Two Roles* (1956) Alva Myrdal and Viola Klein showed that women lacked equal work opportunities. They demanded more training for older women returning to paid work, extended maternity leave, better child care and shorter working hours for both parents – foreshadowing the Women's Liberation campaigns after 1968. It seems that the 1950s was not quite the dull, grey decade often depicted.

* * *

The period between 1945 and the mid-1970s was an unprecedented 'golden age' of near-full employment and rising living standards, though the benefits were not universal: there was periodic unemployment in regions such as Clydeside and Merseyside, and regional inequalities in income and health. Pay and work conditions improved, notably in the large, key industries nationalized by the post-war Attlee government: coal, iron, steel and railways. Almost everyone had two weeks' annual holiday with pay. For the first time, retirement at 60 or 65 became normal, providing an unprecedented period of leisure in later life.

Women had access to a wider range of jobs, but were still limited in pay and had fewer opportunities for promotion and training. This caused growing protest in the 1960s and 1970s, leading to the 1970 Equal Pay Act and the 1975 Sex Discrimination Act. Inequalities diminished but remained significant to the end of the century.

This was the heyday of the long, stable marriage, with life expectancy rising and divorce hard to obtain. Most women married and had children at earlier ages than before. Families remained small – averaging 2.5 children – and most women expected to return to work as their children grew.

The Attlee government did much to reconstruct the

post-war economy and made a brave but incomplete attempt to construct a 'welfare state'. However, by the mid-1950s it was clear that much poverty remained. The Labour governments of 1964–70 attempted to carry forward the Attlee legacy, introducing comprehensive education.

The next twenty-five years were quite different. Following the 'oil shock' of 1973 and growing international economic stability, unemployment rose, remaining high for over twenty years and fuelling fears that the British economy was failing to compete in Europe, the US, and increasingly Asia.

In response, the Conservative governments of the 1980s sought to reconstruct the economy. As a result, the manufacturing industry declined, causing growing unemployment and cultural dislocation in industrial areas.

The twenty-five years between 1975 and 2000 saw significant demographic changes too. The birth rate declined, divorce soared, fewer people married and cohabitation became socially acceptable. By the end of the 1980s one-third of babies were born to unmarried, often cohabiting partners.

The unified British state was also breaking up. Conflict in Northern Ireland between Roman Catholic Nationalists who sought a unified Ireland and Protestant Unionists raged from 1968 until the end of the century. Nationalist movements in Wales and Scotland led to the election in 1999 of devolved assemblies, with considerable control over domestic affairs.

OTHER KEY DATES IN THIS PERIOD

1960 **'Supermac' visits South Africa.** Prime Minister Harold Macmillan tells the South African Parliament that 'a wind of change is blowing through the continent' and Reverend Trevor Huddleston establishes the British anti-apartheid movement, yet this doesn't stop police killing sixty-seven Africans at an anti-apartheid meeting at Sharpeville.

1964 **Wilson wins the general election.** After thirteen long years in the wilderness Labour, led by Harold Wilson, returned to government with a majority of just four seats. It wasn't all plain sailing for Wilson. Labour Shadow Foreign Secretary Patrick Gordon Walker was defeated in Smethwick in an election campaign dogged by allegations of racism; in fact, the battle for the Smethwick seat was so bitter that Wilson described the eventual victor Peter Griffiths as a 'parliamentary leper'.

1968 **Anti-war marches spark violence.** Four years of increasingly bloody conflict in Vietnam led to a series of huge anti-war demonstrations in cities across the world. London's march centred around the home of the US ambassador to Britain on Grosvenor Square, and culminated in clashes between the protesters and police.

1973 **Britain joins the EEC.** Prime Minister Edward Heath finally took Britain into Europe after two previous applications to join (in 1963 and 1967) were rejected by the French president De Gaulle.

1979 **Economic gloom descends.** As the decade neared its end, Britain found itself in the grip of the 'winter of discontent', marked by crippling strikes, the 'three-day week' and growing unemployment. This spelt disaster for Jim Callaghan's Labour government, and he was replaced by Britain's first female prime minister, Margaret Thatcher.

1982 **Falklands War.** On 2 April 1982, Britain was rocked by the news that Argentinian forces had seized the Falkland Islands, ending 150 years of British rule. A task force of over 100 ships and 27,000 personnel was hastily dispatched and wrested control of the island from Argentinian dictator General Galtieri in a conflict that cost hundreds of lives. Hostilities formally ceased on 20 June, by which time Galtieri had resigned.

1989 **End of the Cold War.** The USSR's policy of glasnost (openness) inspired risings against Communist leadership in Eastern Europe. Mass movements through the Iron Curtain culminated in Berliners destroying the wall that had divided the city since 1961.

1997 **Tony Blair wins by a landslide.** The Labour Party, led by Tony Blair, ended eighteen years of Conservative rule with victory in the general election. One of Blair's first acts as prime minister was to join forces with US President Clinton to persuade the IRA to act as a political party rather than a fighting force. Blair's first few months in office were also marked by the death of Princess Diana in a car crash in Paris. Diana's death caused a remarkable outpouring of national grief. Blair went on to be Labour's longest-serving prime minister.

1999 **First elections for Scottish Parliament and Welsh Assembly.** The minimum wage was also introduced this year. The Metropolitan Police was accused of institutional racism in an inquiry into the 1983 death of Stephen Lawrence. In politics, the number of hereditary peers allowed to participate in the work of the House of Lords was reduced to ninety-two.

AFTERWORD

Evolution of the nation

CHRISTOPHER LEE

We all recognize important moments in the lives and identity of our family. So it is with a nation: the birth of a dynasty; the marriage of movements; the old order changing. For each chapter in this book, an eminent historian was asked to choose the key year in a half-century of British history. In effect the work became a collective pursuit for the enigma of Britishness.

Britishness is how we see ourselves and how others see us. Therefore, Britishness depends on whether we play up to our image and have a reasonable understanding of our history and its supporting values. This presents no difficulty for Scots, Irish and Welsh. Having Scottish roots (my mother was a Robertson), I understand my identity, particularly on the day of the Calcutta Cup when I fly the saltire from the upper yard of my boat. The comedian's opening routine of 'There was an Englishman, Irishman and a Scotsman . . .' (the Welsh rarely get in here) tells us immediately our perceived character identities. Furthermore, that we would subconsciously judge the historical position of each country according to our own nationality is self-evident.

For historical reasons the Welsh, Irish and Scots have a largely common view of the English whereas the English have quite differing views of each of the other three. The English saw themselves as masters and the others as simply three more nations they had put down. And here, this project gets close to the confusion about Britishness and national identity: Britishness is of course, Englishness.

Noel Coward described 'the Englishman with his usual bloody cold', meaning the stuffy, almost upper class, stiff upper lip and sniffing colonial servant – the stereotype of all that was British. The British were fair, urbane, sinisterly self-deprecating and most of all, undemonstrative. The rich sent their children away to school playingfields in order to win later battles. The less well-off aspired to be middle class and used the aristocracy as models of style and nature so that they too practised Britishness.

However, Britishness is a recent definition. Those who caused the turning points in British history could not, until well into the millennium, be called British anyway, not even what we now understand to be English. The Danish (and let us not forget the Norwegian) raids of the late eighth century had, by the ninth and tenth centuries, resulted in conquest and settlement in East Anglia, Northumbria and Mercia at a time when England had become for the first time a single state. Until Æthelstan (924–39) and then Edgar (959–75), a monarch ruled the people but not necessarily the state. When Cnut arrived in 1016 there was a sense of distinct kingdoms and peoples. Duncan and then Macbeth ruled Scotland (or Scotia), Gruffudd ap Llywelyn dominated in Powys and Gwynedd until overwhelmed by Harold of Wessex and his brother Tostig (1063). Ireland, split into mini-kingdoms, was by the twelfth century identifiable, at least culturally, as a nation.

The arrival of William and his Normans did nothing to

change the balance of these islands. England was the superpower and, in that tradition, it was to the twelfth-century
Norman knights of Pembroke that Dermot MacMurrough
turned to save his Irish throne. It took months to find
Henry II, the first Angevin, to get his permission for the
intervention in Ireland because he was looking after his
interests in France.

The French connection is relevant to the story of these
islands. For centuries, regions of France were English
owned or leased and the English court spoke French as
natives until the fifteenth century. The connection was
distinct in the origins and the continuity of the Hundred
Years War (1337–1453). There were so many blood, territorial and language ties that it was all but a civil war. In
1453, the English with their Welsh archers were left with
only Calais as a stronghold in France. By this point, the
English identity was more clearly understood (as was the
French).

As John Guy shows in his chapter covering the first half
of the sixteenth century, it was Henry VIII's purpose to
take control of Britain. It was Henry who joined his nation
with the Holy League against France (1511). This was the
time of the Battle of the Spurs, the death of James IV at
Flodden, Luther's attack on indulgences and the spread of
the Reformation. Later, Henry talked of the British Empire
– meaning that his lands were beyond the rule of the pope
– and the British people. Certain events give us the first
great sense of the complexities of nationalism, but not
Britishness: the Reformation Parliament (1529–36); the
Act in Restraint of Appeals; Acts of Succession and Act of
Supremacy; suppression of the monasteries and Henry's
assumption as head of State and Church in Ireland.

Britishness also has its historical base in exploration.
The British image overseas, especially from the seventeenth century, has much to do with how the world still

views the peoples of these islands. Yet the British were hardly the first to step ashore in others' lands and to plant flags of annexation. It was not until the later 1500s that the British started to catch the Portuguese, Dutch and Spanish in global exploration. (The Cabots' fifteenth-century voyages certainly left no colonial footprint). It was as an island race and 'seafaring nation' that the British identity developed both at home and abroad.

Pauline Croft chose the truly heaven-sent defeat of the Armada (1588) as the key year for the second half of the sixteenth century. This triumph endorsed Britain's maritime status and control of its immediate sea lanes more effectively than any naval victory since Sluys (1340). Drake and his like impressed the seal of England on parts of the world that would one day be Britain's imperial adventure playground.

The German traveller Paul Hentzner described late Elizabethan London as being the centre of the British Empire (he meant the capital of all Britain owned) and was much impressed on his journey from Rye with the manner of the English, whom he saw as confident people, slightly aloof, with a liking for drink and too much sugar. In short, even towards the end of the sixteenth century, there was an Englishness – if not a Britishness – that we might find recognizable today. Moreover, national animosities were then crystal clear.

When James I and VI used the term Great Britain to describe the union of his crowns he did not disguise the cool reception his Scottish courtiers received from the sniffy Englishmen. Yet this disdain for others was no more remarkable than the disdain of aristocracy anywhere in the world for those of a different cultural and social breed.

Rab Houston's description of the Scottish rebellion against Charles I and archbishop Laud demonstrates the frustration of the other islanders against the English and their Britishness. By sheer numbers, organization and wealth, the English would always win, especially against those who were inevitably disorganized, had fewer people and no money. Britishness, then, included the arrogance of overwhelming military opposition and putting the vanquished in their social places.

Like any nation, the British identified with their victors and often-imagined saviours. Yet in the British character there is also that special talent for knocking down heroes. Ralegh was a favourite but when he went to Winchester for his trial in November 1603 his carriage was stoned. Marlborough was accused of misappropriation of funds. Clive was disparaged. Hastings was impeached. Raffles was derided – although Singapore and the London Zoo are not bad memorials. Nelson was an exception: he was adored by the masses so none dared mock him and the toast in the Royal Navy remains to the Immortal Memory.

The British – all four nations – have always liked their naval heroes. It has something to do with the British belief that it is their God-given right to roam the seas. So James Thomson (a Scot, remember) wrote 'Rule, Britannia', that England should rule the waves by God's comman'. There we have it: if there is something called Britishness, then God approves.

In the nineteenth century, the Industrial Revolution only confirmed that there may have been none so fair as the British grenadier and none so strong as those with hearts of oak, but the true superiority that the British claimed was in its innovations. Engineers governed the quarter of the world that Britannia ruled by 1900. Peter Mandler's chapter on the Great Exhibition of 1851 transforming Britain into something without compare surely captures the spirit of Britishness.

A hundred years later (and another exhibition, the Festival of Britain, 1951) and they were still singing that

British was best and therefore Britishness was all about being superior. It was a superiority of the whole nation that continued to be governed as it had been since Magna Carta – by its aristocracy. Harold Macmillan said of Lord Carrington that he was an asset because if he did not like what was going on he could always 'bugger off back to his estates'. Robert Menzies (former Australian prime minister) thought that was what Britishness was about: independence of mind with a sense of duty. Equally, Britishness included a fear that individuals would get above themselves. Horace Pendyce in Galsworthy's *The Country House*, set in the 1890s, was long convinced that 'individualism had ruined England and he had set himself deliberately to eradicate this vice from the character of his tenants.'

Pendyce's rural world would struggle until a twenty-first-century squire, pockets full of bonuses or Gazprom share certificates, settled into the big houses of Britain. But they would not represent Britishness because they sought nothing more than the illusion of the sanctuary of Britishness. Maybe it began to fade with Pat Thane's last charge of imperialism at Suez in 1956, although it really started with the disillusionment of the post-Second World War period, in spite of the social revolution. Crucially, the post-Suez generation produced a society that wasted then abandoned the huge strides in education of R.A. Butler and Ellen Wilkinson. One consequence is that the English now apologize for their history rather than study it. Without history there is no need of identification. This is the real English disease.

All this suggests that if the 'Turning Points' series – first and foremost wonderful storytelling – was taught as a school history course it would excite a new generation. Let me quote just one line from Jeremy Black's piece on the year 1776: 'American independence permanently transformed the nature of the British Empire.' That sentence prompts so many questions. It would launch a class into 200 years of the history of our immediate and very traceable ancestors. Would we find who we are today? Of course not. That's something for the next generation to explore.

FURTHER READING

Introduction

Wood, Michael, *In Search of England* (Penguin, 1999).

Wood, Michael, 'Stand Firm Against the Monsters', in Jinty Nelson (ed.), *Lay Intellectuals in the Carolingian World* (Cambridge University Press, 2007).

1016 The Danish Conquest of England

Lavelle, Ryan, *Ethelred II: King of the English* (Tempus, 2002).

Lawson, M.K., Cnut: The Danes in England in the Early 11th Century (Longman, 1993).

Rumble, A.R. (ed.), *The Reign of Cnut: King of England, Denmark and Norway* (Leicester University Press, 1994).

Stenton, F.M., *Anglo-Saxon England* (Oxford University Press, 1971).

1066 William and the Normans arrive

Barlow, Frank, *The Godwins: The Rise and Fall of a Noble Dynasty* (Longman, 2002).

Bates, David, *William the Conqueror* (Tempus, 2004).

Higham, Nicholas, *The Death of Anglo-Saxon England* (Sutton, 1997).

John, E., 'The Return of the Vikings' and 'The End of Anglo-Saxon England', in James Campbell (ed.), *The Anglo-Saxons* (Penguin, 1991).

Maund, Kari, *The Welsh Kings: The Medieval Rulers of Wales* (Tempus, 2000).

Williams, Ann, *The English and the Norman Conquest* (Boydell, 1995).

1141 Stephen and Matilda fight a civil war

Chibnall, Marjorie, *The Empress Matilda* (Blackwell, 1991).
Crouch, David, *The Reign of King Stephen* (Longman, 2000).
King, Edmund (ed.), *William of Malmesbury, 'Historia Novella':
The Contemporary History* (Oxford Medieval Texts, 1998).

1171 Henry II invades Ireland

Duffy, Sean, *Ireland in the Middle Ages* (Palgrave Macmillan,
1996).
Duggan, Anne, *Thomas Becket* (Hodder Arnold, 2004).
Frame, Robin, *Colonial Ireland, 1169–1369* (Helicon, 1981).
Gillingham, John, *The English in the Twelfth Century* (Boydell,
2003).

1215 Magna Carta is forced on John

Carpenter, David, *The Struggle for Mastery: The Penguin History
of Britain, 1066–1284* (Penguin Paperback, 2004).
Holt, J.C., *Magna Carta* (Cambridge University Press, 1992).
Holt, J.C., *The Northerners. A Study in the Reign of King John*
(Oxford University Press, 1961).
Warren, W.L., *King John* (Yale University Press, 1997).

1295 Edward I goes on the warpath

Morris, Marc, *A Great and Terrible King. Edward I and the Forging of Britain* (Hutchinson, 2008).
Prestwich, Michael, *Edward I* (Yale University Press, 1997).
Prestwich, Michael, *The Three Edwards: War and State in England, 1272–1377* (Routledge, 2003).

1348 The Black Death hits Britain

Horrox, Rosemary (ed.), *The Black Death* (Manchester Univer-
sity Press, 1994).
Ormrod, Mark, and Phillip Lindley (eds), *The Black Death in
England* (Paul Watkins, 1996).

Prestwich, Michael, *Plantagenet England, 1225–1360* (Oxford University Press, 2005).

1381 Peasants rise in revolt

Dobson, R.B. (ed.), *The Peasants' Revolt of 1381* (Macmillan,1983) (a collection of all the contemporary accounts in translation).
Dunn, Alastair, *The Great Rising of 1381* (Tempus, 2004).

1415 Henry V takes the field at Agincourt

Allmand, Christopher, *Henry V* (Yale University Press, 1997).
Curry, Anne, *Agincourt* (Tempus, 2005).
Griffiths, Ralph (ed.), *Short Oxford History of the British Isles: The Fourteenth and Fifteenth Centuries* (Oxford University Press, 2003).
Harriss, Gerald, *Shaping the Nation: England, 1360–1461* (Oxford University Press, 2005).

1483 Richard III snatches the crown

Carpenter, Christine, *The Wars of the Roses: Politics and the Constitution in England c. 1437–1509* (Cambridge University Press, 1997).
Castor, Helen, *Blood and Roses: The Paston Family and the Wars of the Roses* (Faber and Faber, 2004).
Dyer, Christopher, *An Age of Transition? Economy and Society in England in the Later Middle Ages* (Oxford University Press, 2005).
Horrox, Rosemary, *Richard III: A Study of Service* (Cambridge University Press, 1989).
Rigby, S.H. (ed.), *A Companion to Britain in the Later Middle Ages* (Blackwell, 2003).

1534 Henry VIII tries to take control of Britain

Armitage, David, *The Ideological Origins of the British Empire* (Cambridge University Press, 2000).

Ellis, Steven, *Tudor Frontiers and Noble Power: The Making of the British State* (Oxford University Press, 1995).

Mason, Roger, *Kingship and Commonweal: Political Thought in Renaissance and Reformation Scotland* (Tuckwell Press, 1998).

1588 The Armada is repelled

Doran, Susan, and Glen Richardson, *Tudor England and its Neighbours* (Palgrave Macmillan, 2005).

Martin, Colin, and Geoffrey Parker, *The Spanish Armada* (revised edition, Penguin, 1999).

Rodriguez-Salgado, M.J., and Simon Adams (eds), *England, Spain and the Gran Armada 1585-1604* (John Donald, 1991).

1638 Scots revolt against Charles I

Kenyon, John, and Jane Ohlmeyer (eds), *The Civil Wars: A Military History of England, Scotland, and Ireland 1638-1660* (Oxford University Press, 1998).

Macinnes, Allan, *The British Revolution, 1629-1660* (Palgrave Macmillan, 2004).

Russell, Conrad, *The Fall of the British Monarchies, 1637-1642* (Clarendon Press, 1991).

1662 Charles II pays a heavy price for his Restoration

Harris, Tim, *Restoration: Charles II and his Kingdoms* (Penguin, 2004).

Hutton, Ronald, *The Restoration: A Political and Religious History of England and Wales 1658-1667* (Oxford University Press, 1985).

Keeble, N.H., *The Restoration: England in the 1660s* (Blackwell, 2002).

1745 The Jacobites rebel

Black, Jeremy, *Culloden and the '45* (Sutton Publishing, 2000).

McLynn, Frank, *Charles Edward Stuart. A Tragedy in Many Acts* (Routledge, 1988).

Szechi, Daniel, *The Jacobites. Britain and Europe 1688–1788* (Manchester University Press, 1994).

1776 America declares independence from the motherland

Black, Jeremy, *Eighteenth-Century Britain* (Palgrave, 2001).

Langford, Paul, *A Polite and Commercial People: England, 1727–1783* (Oxford University Press, 1989).

Prest, Wilfred, *Albion Ascendant. English History 1660–1815* (Oxford University Press, 1998).

1832 The Reform Bill is passed

Brock, Michael, *The Great Reform Act* (Hutchinson, 1973).

Evans, Eric, *The Forging of the Modern State: Early Industrial Britain* (3rd edition, Longman, 2001).

Hall, Catherine, 'The Rule of Difference: Gender, Class and Empire in the Making of the 1832 Reform Act', in Ida Blom et al. (eds), *Gendered Nations. Nationalisms and Gender Order in the Long Nineteenth Century* (Berg, 2000).

Thompson, E.P. *The Making of the English Working Class* (Penguin, 1968).

1851 The Great Exhibition transforms Britain

Auerbach, Jeffrey, *The Great Exhibition of 1851: A Nation on Display* (Yale University Press, 1999).

Briggs, Asa, *Victorian People: A Reassessment of Persons and Themes 1851–67* (1954; Penguin, 1990).

Piggott, J.R., *Palace of the People: The Crystal Palace at Sydenham, 1854–1936* (Hurst & Co., 2004).

1916 The Somme, and Lloyd George founds his coalition

Addison, Paul, *The Road to 1945* (Pimlico, 1994).

DeGroot, Gerard, *Blighty: British Society in the Era of the Great War* (Longman, 1996).

Hennessy, Peter, *Never Again* (Penguin, 2006).

Pugh, Martin, *The Making of Modern British Politics 1867–1945* (Blackwell, 2002).

1956 Suez signals the dying days of empire

Butler, David, and Gareth Butler, *Twentieth Century British Political Facts, 1900–2000* (Macmillan, 2000).

Clarke, Peter, *Land of Hope and Glory. Britain, 1900–1990*, (Penguin, 1996).

Halsey, A.H., and Josephine Webb (eds), *Twentieth Century British Social Trends* (Macmillan, 2000).

Reynolds, David, *One World Divisible: A Global History since 1945* (Penguin, 2000).

Thane, Pat, *Cassell's Companion to Twentieth Century Britain* (Cassell, 2001).

CONTRIBUTORS

Caroline Barron is Professor of the History of London at Royal Holloway, University of London. Her most recent book is *London in the Later Middle Ages: Government and People* (Oxford University Press, 2004).

Jeremy Black is Professor of History at the University of Exeter. His vast number of books include *A History of the British Isles* (2nd edition, Palgrave, 2002), *The British Seaborne Empire* (Yale University Press, 2004), and *A Short History of Britain* (Social Affairs Unit, 2007).

Christine Carpenter is Professor of Medieval English History at the University of Cambridge. Her books include *Locality and Polity: A Study of Warwickshire Landed Society, 1401–1499* (Cambridge University Press, 1992), and *The Armburgh Papers* (Boydell and Brewer, 1998).

David Carpenter is Professor in Medieval History at King's College London. He is author of The Minority of Henry III (Methuen, 1990), *The Reign of Henry III* (Hambledon, 1996) and *The Struggle for Mastery: The Penguin History of Britain, 1066–1284* (Penguin, 2004).

Pauline Croft is Professor of Early Modern History at Royal Holloway, University of London, and is convenor of the Tudor–Stuart seminar at the Institute of Historical Research, University of London. She edited, and contributed a chapter to, *Patronage, Culture and Power: The Early Cecils, 1558-1612* (Yale, 2002) and is the author of *King James* (Palgrave, 2003).

Gerard DeGroot is Professor of Modern History at St Andrews University. His books include *The Sixties Unplugged: A Kaleidoscopic History of a Disorderly Decade* (Macmillan, 2008).

Sarah Foot is Professor of Ecclesiastical History at Christ Church, Oxford. She is the author of *Monastic Life in Anglo-Saxon England, c. 600–900* (Cambridge University Press, 2006; paperback, 2009), and *Veiled Women* (Ashgate, 2000).

John Guy is a Fellow of Clare College, Cambridge, specializing in the period 1450–1700. He received the 2004 Whitbread Biography Award and Marsh Prize for his biography *My Heart is My Own: The Life of Mary Queen of Scots* (Harper Perennial). His other publications include *Tudor England* (Oxford University Press, 1990).

John Gillingham is Emeritus Professor of History at the London School of Economics. His recent books include *Richard I* (Yale, 1999), *The Angevin Empire* (Hodder, 2001) and *Medieval Britain: A Very Short Introduction* (with Ralph Griffiths; Oxford University Press, 2000).

Ralph Griffiths is Emeritus Professor of Medieval History at Swansea University. His books include *The Reign of King Henry VI* (new edition, Sutton, 1998), and *Medieval Britain: A Very Short Introduction* (with John Gillingham, Oxford University Press, 2000).

Catherine Hall is Professor of Modern British Social and Cultural History at University College, London. She is the author of *Civilising Subjects: Metropole and Colony in the English Imagination, 1830–1867* (University of Chicago Press, 2002) and co-editor of *At Home with the Empire* (with Sonya Rose, Cambridge University Press, 2006)

Nicholas Higham is Professor of Early Medieval and Landscape History at the University of Manchester. His books include *King Arthur: Myth-making and History* (Routledge, 2002), *A Frontier Landscape* (Windgather, 2004) and *(Re-) Reading Bede: The Ecclesiastical History in Context* (Taylor and Francis, 2007).

Rab Houston is Professor of Modern History at the University of St Andrews. His recent books include *A New History of Scotland* (2001) and *Scotland: A Very Short Introduction* (Oxford University Press, 2008).

Edmund King is Emeritus Professor of Medieval History at the University of Sheffield. He is editor of *The Anarchy of King Stephen's Reign* (Oxford, 1994) and author of *Medieval England, from Hastings to Bosworth* (The History Press, 2009).

Christopher Lee was the first Quatercentenary Fellow in Contemporary History at Emmanuel College, Cambridge, and is researching the history of ideas at Birkbeck College, London. He is the author of the BBC Radio 4 history of Britain, *This Sceptred Isle*, and the forthcoming *History of Britishness* (Constable, 2010).

Peter Mandler is Reader in Modern British History at Gonville and Caius College, Cambridge. He is the author of *The English National Character: The History of an Idea from Edmund Burke to Tony Blair* (Yale University Press, 2006).

John Morrill is Professor of British and Irish History at the University of Cambridge. His research interests lie in the political, religious, social and cultural histories of England, Ireland and Scotland in the early modern period.

W. Mark Ormrod is Professor of History at the University of York. He is the author of *The Reign of Edward III* (revised edition, Tempus, 2000), and co-editor of *The Parliament Rolls of Medieval England* (Boydell and Brewer, 2005) and *A Social*

History of England, 1200–1500 (Cambridge University Press, 2006).

Michael Prestwich is Emeritus Professor of History at the University of Durham. He has written extensively on thirteenth- and fourteenth-century history and his latest book is *Plantagenet England 1225–1360* (Oxford University Press, 2005).

Daniel Szechi is Professor of Early Modern British History at the University of Manchester. His most recent book is *1715. The Great Jacobite Rebellion* (Yale University Press, 2006).

Pat Thane is Professor of Contemporary British History, and Director of the Centre for Contemporary British History, Institute of Historical Research, University of London. Her books include *The Foundations of the Welfare State* (Longman, 1996).

Michael Wood is a highly respected author and TV presenter and is a Fellow of the Royal Historical Society. He has over eighty documentary films to his name, most recently the critically acclaimed *The Story of India*.